BUSINESS PRACTICES, GROWTH AND ECONOMIC POLICY IN EMERGING MARKETS

WSPC Series in Business and Emerging Markets

Series Editor: Satyendra Singh *(University of Winnipeg, Canada)*

Developing countries and emerging markets have one of the fastest growth rates around the world given the advancement in technology, rise in global investments, and change in culture. So the knowledge translation and transfer from advanced countries to emerging markets and vice-versa is of essence; the advanced countries need access to the markets of emerging markets and the emerging markets need the technology and investments, among others, from advanced countries. It is a win-win situation. In this context, the WSPC book series in association with the Academy of Business and Emerging Markets (ABEM) invite research studies based on controversial and/or thought-provoking topics yet theoretically sound from authors based in developing countries and emerging markets to contribute to the book on any of following three broad research areas — business, government, and community — however the chapters must relate to title of the book, i.e. business practices, growth and economic policies in emerging markets

Published

Vol. 1   *Business Practices, Growth and Economic Policy in Emerging Markets*
          edited by Luis Camacho and Satyendra Singh

WSPC Series in Business and Emerging Markets

BUSINESS PRACTICES, GROWTH AND ECONOMIC POLICY IN EMERGING MARKETS

Editors

Luis Camacho
SUNY Empire State College, USA

Satyendra Singh
University of Winnipeg, Canada

World Scientific

NEW JERSEY · LONDON · SINGAPORE · BEIJING · SHANGHAI · HONG KONG · TAIPEI · CHENNAI · TOKYO

Published by

World Scientific Publishing Co. Pte. Ltd.

5 Toh Tuck Link, Singapore 596224

USA office: 27 Warren Street, Suite 401-402, Hackensack, NJ 07601

UK office: 57 Shelton Street, Covent Garden, London WC2H 9HE

Library of Congress Cataloging-in-Publication Data
Names: Camacho, Luis A., editor. | Singh, Satyendra, 1966–   editor.
Title: Business practices, growth and economic policy in emerging markets / editors, Luis Camacho,
    SUNY Empire State College, USA, Satyendra Singh, University of Winnipeg, Canada.
Description: USA : World Scientific, 2020. | Series: WSPC series in
    business and emerging markets ; vol. 1 | Includes index.
Identifiers: LCCN 2020028247 | ISBN 9789811221743 (hardcover) |
    ISBN 9789811221750 (ebook) | ISBN 9789811221767 (ebook other)
Subjects: LCSH: International business enterprises--Developing countries. |
    Industrial management--Developing countries. | Economic development--
    Developing countries. | Developing countries--Economic policy.
Classification: LCC HD2932 .B877 2020 | DDC 338.9009172/4--dc23
LC record available at https://lccn.loc.gov/2020028247

British Library Cataloguing-in-Publication Data
A catalogue record for this book is available from the British Library.

For any available supplementary material, please visit
https://www.worldscienti ic.com/worldscibooks/10.1142/11863#t=suppl

Desk Editors: Aanand Jayaraman/Sandhya Venkatesh

Typeset by Stallion Press
Email: enquiries@stallionpress.com

Printed in Singapore

Preface

In the past two decades, developing countries and emerging markets have exhibited extraordinary growth representing about half of global gross domestic product (GDP); therefore, developed countries no longer control the world economy. At the same time, emerging markets have witnessed a significant socioeconomic and political transformation, although limited public spending, poor governance, corruption, poverty and inequality persist across the markets. Despite rapid growth in emerging markets, their population remains significantly poorer than developed countries.

Changes in the geopolitical environment require corporations operating in international business to adopt a culture of innovation and diversity as a corporate strategy. In this context, the Academy of Business and Emerging Markets (ABEM), Canada in association with World Scientific Publishers, Singapore, recognizing the importance of analyzing and measuring the dynamic of these emerging markets, decided to disseminate the knowledge through the book entitled *Business Practices, Growth and Economic Policy in Emerging Markets*. It is part of our commitment to encourage and support scholars to investigate topics that generate knowledge in emerging markets relating to the private and public sectors to create business strategies and public policies that will benefit these markets.

For the book, we received 16 chapters from 12 countries fulfilling the aim and expectations of the book — a broad variety of chapters. Out of these chapters, we selected only eight chapters from eight countries through the double-blind peer-review process. These chapters cover essential topics such as market entry strategies, international market expansion, artificial intelligence and cyber security, poverty alleviation, building innovation capacity, talent management, business incubation process and ICT technologies. The book has been written after conducting comprehensive research and has implications for both scholars and practitioners. We feel honored to include the chapters from well-known professors from Australia, China, Croatia, Japan, Mexico, Tunisia, UK and USA. Overall, the book provides a broad vision to academic scholars, business managers and policymakers about the trends and strategies needed to improve business performance in emerging markets.

Indeed, we are grateful to the authors for their contributions; the reviewers for their reviews; University of Winnipeg, SUNY Empire State College and ABEM for their support; and Dr. Zvi Ruder and Ms. Sandhya Venkatesh from the *World Scientific Publishers* for their editorial help.

We hope that you find the book beneficial. We shall look forward to receiving your comments.

Luis Camacho
SUNY Empire State College, NY, USA
luis.camacho@esc.edu

Satyendra Singh
University of Winnipeg, Canada
s.singh@uwinnipeg.ca

About the Editors

Luis Camacho is an Assistant Professor of Business, International Business, and Marketing at SUNY Empire State College. He is Associate Editor of *Journal of the Academy of Business and Emerging Markets* (JABEM) and former Editor Chair of the South American Region for the JABEM. Additionally, he is Editorial Board Member for the *International Journal of Applied Management Science* (IJAMS), Communications Chair and the Caribbean Region for the Academy of Business and Emerging Markets (ABEM). Dr. Camacho's research activity is based on consumer behavior and international marketing, emphasizing ethnocentrism and xenocentrism on consumer purchase intention, productive linkages and global value chains, ethnic markets and corporate citizenship in International Business. Dr. Camacho has published in reputed international journals such as *Sustainability* and presented papers in international conferences as AIB, AIBSE, ABEM and delivered keynotes in different countries. Dr. Camacho can be contacted at *luis.camacho@esc.edu*.

Satyendra Singh is a Professor of Marketing & International Business, Faculty of Business and Economics, University of Winnipeg, Canada, and Editor-in-Chief of *Journal of the Academy of Business and Emerging Markets*, Canada. Dr. Singh's research interests lie in developing countries and emerging markets with particular emphasis on Africa and Asia on issues relating to the impact of transitional governments' economic policies on business performance. Dr. Singh has published widely in reputed journals such as IMR, TIBR, IMI, SIJ, MIP, JSM, JGM and MD among others and has presented papers at international conferences such as AIB, AMA, AM, AMS, ASAC, BAM, EMAC and WMC to list a few. Presently, he is authoring a book on *Luxury and Fashion Marketing,* Routledge, USA. Dr. Singh is a frequent keynote speaker and has traveled over 90 countries to teach, train or consult. Dr. Singh can be contacted at *s.singh@uwinnipeg.ca.*

About the Contributors

Maria Teresa Beamond is an Assistant Professor at RMIT University. Within the human resource management (HRM) and international business fields, Maria's research interest covers international HRM, global talent management, emerging economies, corporate social responsibility and employment relations. Before joining RMIT Maria undertook two years Post-doctoral Scholar and Research Fellow at Penn State University. Maria did her PhD in Management at the Business School, The University of Queensland, Australia. Her doctoral thesis relates to the "Translation of Corporate Talent Management across Subsidiaries in Emerging Economies". Maria has taught in USA, Australia, China and Singapore and presented her research work in several countries at academic and industry conferences in Europe, USA, Latin America and Australia. Currently, Maria teaches Global HRM and Managing International Business Responsibly at the Postgraduate and Undergraduate levels. Maria has more than 16 years of work experience in international business dealing with different organizations in Latin America, Australia and USA. Dr. Beamond can be contacted at *maria.beamond@rmit.edu.au*.

Richard W. Carney is in the Department of Strategy and Entrepreneurship at the China Europe International Business School (CEIBS). His teaching and research interests primarily focus on business–government relations. He has published numerous articles in journals such as the *Journal of Financial Economics, Business and Politics* and the *Review of International Political Economy*. He is also the author of *Contested Capitalism: The Political Origins of Financial Systems* (2009) and is the editor of *Lessons from the Asian Financial Crisis* (2009). Prior to joining CEIBS, he taught at the Australian National University and at the Nanyang Technological University in Singapore. He was also a Jean Monnet Fellow at the European University Institute in Florence, Italy. Dr. Carney can be contacted at *carney.richad@ceibs.edu*.

Roger (Rongxin) Chen is a Professor at the School of Management of the University of San Francisco, USA. He co-founded and served as the founding Co-Editor-in-Chief at the *Journal of Asia Business Studies* (JABS). His research focuses on corporate innovation, new business development, global strategy and competition with emphasis on China. He was a longtime consulting Vice President at the Silicon Valley Business Forum (SBF). Currently, he serves as a Foreign Expert Advisor at the Post-doctor Research Group of China Merchant Group. His research has been published in a variety of journals, including *Academy of Management Journal, Management International Review, Asia Pacific Journal of Management Studies, Journal of Business Horizon, R&D Management*. He has received several research awards including "Abramson Award for Outstanding Article" from Business Economics and several faculty research awards from the School of Management at the University of San Francisco. Dr. Chen can be contacted at *chenr@usfca.edu*.

 **Fatma Choura** is an Associate Professor at High Institute of Computer Science (ISI). She holds a PhD from High Institute of Management of Tunis, Tunisia and the University of Nantes-France. She is affiliated to LIGUE Laboratory, Tunisia, a member of the scientific committee of several national and international conferences and co-author of many scientific papers. She is the academic coordinator of Marketing and Management courses and a member of scientific council at ISI. Her teaching areas are Internet marketing, digital management, entrepreneurship, contemporary consumer behavior and communications. She was faculty advisor of several teams of students in marketing, computer science and entrepreneurship. Her research areas involve mainly digital marketing, social marketing, mobile marketing, e-commerce and communications. Dr. Choura can be contacted at *fatma.choura@isi.utm.tn*.

 **Mirjana Čižmešija** is a Full Professor at the Department of Statistics, Faculty of Economics and Business Zagreb (FEB). Her doctoral thesis titled *Statistical and Methodological Background of Business Tendency Surveys* was defended in 2001 at FEB. Her research interests include business and consumer surveys, statistical methods for management decision-making and business forecasting. She has worked on numerous scientific research projects and published over 100 scientific articles and studies. She has been a reviewer for many respectable international journals such as *Quality & Quantity, Economic Research and The World Economy*. She is a member of the review panels constituted by Croatian Science Foundation and the Swiss National Science Foundation and serves as an editorial board member of several scientific journals and conferences. She was the Head of the Department of statistics and the President of the FEB Graduate Studies Committee. Dr. Čižmešija can be contacted at *mcizmesija@efzg.hr*.

Elaine Farndale is an Associate Professor in Human Resource Management and Associate Director of the School of Labor and Employment Relations, Pennsylvania State University (USA), where she is also Founder and Director of the Center for International Human Resource Studies. Elaine's research focuses primarily on international human resource management, strategic HRM, and HRM and performance. She has published widely from her international collaborations in both the practitioner and academic press and has served as an elected member of the *Academy of Management* HR Division Executive Committee, Co-Editor-in-Chief for *Human Resource Management Journal*, and Associate Editor for *Human Resource Management* and *International Journal of Human Resource Management*. Elaine completed her PhD at Cranfield School of Management (UK) and has worked previously as an HR specialist for several years. Dr. Farndale can be contacted at *euf3@psu.edu.*

Charmine E. J. Härtel is a Distinguished Professor and Strategic Advisor to Head of Department of Management at Monash University Business School in Melbourne, Australia. Professor Härtel is an acknowledged preeminent scholar-practitioner in her field, evidenced by election as a Fellow of the Australian Academy of Social Sciences (ASSA), the (US) Society for Industrial and Organizational Psychology (SIOP), the Australian and New Zealand Academy of Management (ANZAM), the Australian Human Resources Institute (AHRI) and Society for Organizational Behavior in Australia (SOBA). Her awards include the inaugural 2019 HR Academic of the Year Award from the Australian Human Resources Institute; the Australian Psychological Society's Elton Mayo Award for scholarly excellence, the Martin E. P. Seligman Applied Research Award and 19 best paper awards. Her research appears have been published in over 200 publications including leading journals such as *Academy of Management Review, Journal of Applied Psychology, Leadership Quarterly, Human Relations, British Journal of Industrial Relations*, and *Journal of Management*. Dr. Härtel can be contacted at *charmine.hartel@ monash.edu.*

Adam Hepworth earned his PhD from the University of Tennessee, Knoxville in 2019. Prior to pursuing a career in academia, Dr. Hepworth worked in software sales and digital marketing. He is currently Assistant Professor of Marketing at Ohio University. His research interests include frontline employee marketing, services marketing and emerging markets. His interest in emerging markets examines how environmental factors (e.g. regulatory institutions) impact emerging market firms' ability to seek opportunities beyond the home country's borders. Dr. Hepworth's interest in emerging markets stems from his international travels and professional experience in marketing. Dr. Hepworth can be contacted at *hepworth@ohio.edu*.

Kelly Hewett is an Associate Professor of Marketing and Haslam Faculty Research Fellow at the University of Tennessee's Haslam College of Business. She also currently serves as Editor-in-Chief of the *Journal of International Marketing*. Kelly's research works have been published in the *Journal of Marketing*, the *Journal of International Business Studies*, the *Journal of the Academy of Marketing Science*, the *Journal of International Marketing* and the *Journal of Management Studies*, among others. She serves on the ERB for the *Journal of Marketing*, the *Journal of International Business Studies*, the *Journal of the Academy of Marketing Science* and the *International Journal of Research in Marketing*. Kelly has received numerous awards and recognitions for her research, teaching and service. She serves as a member of the boards for the Marketing Strategy and Global Marketing Special Interest Groups for the AMA. Dr. Hewett can be contacted at *khewett@utk.edu*.

Tomomi Imagawa is an Assistant Professor of the Graduate School of the Business Breakthrough University in Tokyo in Japan. She received her PhD in commerce from the University of Osaka in 2020. Her academic works mainly relate to studying key success factors of firms from advanced economies and applying them to develop firms based in emerging markets through the perspectives of institution and cultural differences. Dr. Imagawa can be contacted at *tomomi.imagawa@gmail.com.*

Hanna Klarner is a recent Bachelor of Science graduate in International Business from Reutlingen University at the faculty ESB Business School. She has focused specifically in the areas of finance and accounting during her studies. As part of an internship in a London-based portfolio company for start-ups in the research field and during her exchange semester at Tecnológico de Monterrey in Guadalajara, Mexico, she has developed a deep interest in entrepreneurship. She has work experience in finance, management accounting and controlling, as well as consulting in the areas of corporate finance and performance management but is planning to continue pursuing her academic career in fall 2021. She can be contacted at *hanna.klarner@gmail.com.*

Alexander V. Krasnikov is a faculty at Quinlan School of Business, Loyola University of Chicago and research scholar at Center for Research Technology and Innovation Kellogg School of Management, Northwestern University. His expertise falls in the areas of financial impact of marketing, brand equity, evolution of brands and marketing in the emerging markets. He specializes in application of Big Data techniques in the analysis of the branding strategies using trademarks and other forms of Intellectual Property (IP). More generally, he examines complex impact of various forms of IP on the value of firms. Dr. Krasnikov can be contacted at *akrasnikov@luc.edu.*

Thomas Matheus holds a PhD from Warwick University and is a senior lecturer with Northumbria University. He has over 27 years of business, management, research and higher education experience. His career demonstrates a wide-ranging ability to hold managerial responsibility: regional, EU and international — operations management for C&A and subsidiaries; consulting for Retail Consult GmbH and Enabler GmbH (now Wipro) as well as development and management roles in UK universities. Thomas has experience across academic teaching, research and income generation, drawing on and building strategic and sustainable networks internally, locally and internationally. Dr. Matheus can be contacted at *thomas.matheus@northumbria.ac.uk.*

Koichi Nakagawa is an Associate Professor of the Graduate School of Economics at Osaka University, Japan. He received a PhD in economics from the University of Tokyo in 2008. His academic works are mainly about the management of innovation, and his current interests focus on the key success factors for innovation in emerging situations, such as university–industry collaboration, post-corporate acquisition and low-income countries. Recent research can be seen in *Competitiveness Review,* *Technology Innovation Management Review* and *Cross-cultural Management Journal.* He got awarded at ITMC in 2019, ABEM in 2017 and EAMSA and AJBS in 2016. At the same time, he works as a YouTuber (!), a lecturer and a consultant to help entrepreneurs take actions, ranging from the development of sustainable business in Cambodia to acceleration of technological startups in Japan. His personal mission is "Bridging between academy and society". Dr. Nakagawa can be contacted at *nakagawa@econ.osaka-u.ac.jp.*

Miguel Angel Gil Robles is a Research Professor of Accounting and Finance at Tecnologico de Monterrey, Mexico. His academic background is a BA in accounting and finance and an MA in finance, both degrees from Tecnologico de Monterrey. He holds a PhD in accounting and finance from the University of Manchester. His research interests focus on management accounting, organizational learning and management control systems in hi-tech industries. Dr. Robles can be contacted at *m.gil@tec.mx*.

Sihem Ben Saad is an Assistant Professor of Marketing at the Carthage Business School of the University of Tunis Carthage (UTC), Tunisia. She holds a PhD in marketing from the Institute of Higher Business Studies of Carthage (IHEC Carthage). Before joining UTC, she held faculty positions at the Higher School of Communications of Tunis (Supcom Tunis), Higher Institute of Computer Science (ISI Tunis) and Higher Institute of Technological Studies of Communications of Tunis (ISET'COM). Her research interests include digital marketing and child behavior. Dr. Saad taught a variety of courses such as Introduction to Marketing, Consumer Behavior, Project Management, Entrepreneurship and Corporate Culture. Dr. Saad has presented papers at several national and international conferences such as the French Association of Marketing (AFM) and the Tunisian Association of Marketing (ATM). Dr. Saad can be contacted at *sihem.bensaad87@gmail.com*.

Meera Sarma is the Director of Studies for the Online DBA (Doctor of Business Administration) at University of Liverpool. She has held previous roles in leading doctoral programs and various academic positions. She has extensive experience of working in consulting roles with a focus on technology, virtual knowledge networks, cyber security and specifically online extremism and cyber terrorism. She received a PhD from Royal Holloway, University of London. Her main areas of research are innovation in cyber space, virtual communities software development and open source software innovation. She has a particular interest in hackers, online extremism, cyber terrorism and artificial intelligence. Dr. Sarma can be contacted at *meera.sarma@liverpool.ac.uk.*

Chaminda Senaratne's research interests are in the areas of resources and capabilities perspectives of strategic management and entrepreneurial capabilities of high-tech SMEs. Before joining NBS in 2013, he worked as a member of the visiting faculty and a research assistant at the School of Management, Royal Holloway, and University of London. He holds a PhD in management and a Postgraduate Diploma in Skills of Teaching to Inspire Learning from Royal Holloway, University of London. He is an Associate Fellow of the Higher Education Academy, UK. Dr. Senaratne can be contacted at *chaminda.senaratne@northumbria.ac.uk.*

Tihana Škrinjarić is an Assistant Professor at the Department of Mathematics at the Faculty of Economics and Business of the University of Zagreb. Her research areas are risk management, econometrics and financial economics with special focus on portfolio management. She has published over 100 publications in these research areas and participated in dozens of international conferences on econometrics and operational research. Dr. Škrinjarić has been a member of the Croatian Operational Research Society and the Croatian Statistical Association. Dr. Škrinjarić can be contacted at *tskrinjar@net.efzg.hr.*

Xiaohua Yang is a Professor of International Business and the Director of China Business Studies Initiative at the University of San Francisco. She has published numerous referred journal articles on the topics of internationalization of firms, international R&D strategic alliances, corporate social responsibility in multinational corporations and innovation. She has taught and lectured in the USA, Australia, China, Taiwan and Europe. She is a recipient of multiple best conference paper awards and has received three outstanding research awards from the USF School of Management. She has served as a Guest Editor for several international journals, including *Asia Pacific Journal of Management*, *Business Ethics Quarterly*, *Multinational Business Review* and *Thunderbird International Business Review*. Dr. Yang can be contacted at *yuxiyulu@126.com*.

 **Ying Zhou** is a Lecturer at the School of Business of Nanjing Audit University. She got the Bachelor and Master's degree from Southeast University in China and doctoral degree from Queensland University of Technology in Australia. Her research focuses on regional innovation capacity and has been published in journals such as *International Journal of Innovation Management* and *International Journal of Technological Learning Innovation and Development*. She has served for International Association for Chinese Management Research as the Assistant to Editor-in-Chief. She has worked on projects of international collaboration between Nanjing Audit University and Arizona State University. Dr. Zhou can be contacted at *yuxiyulu@126.com*.

List of Chapter Reviewers

Luis Baquero, Pontificia Universidad Catolica de Puerto Rico

Jose Brache, University of Auckland, New Zealand

Luis Camacho, SUNY Empire State College, USA

Miguel Cerna, Donghua University, China

Janette Chaljub, Universidad del Caribe. Dominican Republic

Valerie Chukhlomin, SUNY Empire State College

Bonageres Dominguez, Instituto Tecnologico de Santo Domingo (INTEC), Dominican Republic

Alvaro García, Universidad Estatal a Distancia (UNED), Costa Rica

Angelina Galvez-Kiser, University of the Incarnate Word, USA

Velia Govaere, Universidad Estatal a Distancia (UNED), Costa Rica

Thomas Kernodle, SUNY Empire State College, USA

Dongho Kim, SUNY Empire State College, USA

Edith Moya, Universidad del Caribe. Dominican Republic

Koichi Nakagawa, Osaka University, Japan

Fernando Parrado, Universidad Sergio Arboleda, Colombia

Michael Pasco, San Beda University, Philippines

Marius Potgieter, North-West University, South Africa

Julio Ramírez, Universidad Pontificia Bolivariana, Colombia

Patricio Ramirez, Universidad Catolica del Norte, Chile

Meena Rambocas, University of West Indies, Trinidad and Tobago

Cristian Salazar, Universidad Austral de Chile, Chile
Meera Sarma, University of Liverpool, UK
Satyendra Singh, University of Winnipeg, Canada
Greibin Villegas, Universidad Estatal a Distancia (UNED), Costa Rica
Jose Rojas-Mendez, Carleton University, Canada

Contents

Chapter 1

Introduction

Satyendra Singh[*,‡] and Luis Camacho[†,§]

*University of Winnipeg, Winnipeg, MB R3B 2E9, Canada

†SUNY Empire State College, Staten Island, NY 10305, USA

‡s.singh@uwinnipeg.ca

§luis.camacho@esc.edu

This book contains eight chapters from eight countries — Australia, China, Croatia, Japan, Mexico, Tunisia, UK and USA. In the lead chapter, Hewett, Krasnikov and Hepworth examine the impact of home market institutional conditions on market entry strategies of firms from emerging markets. The authors explore the extent to which the regulatory institutional environment, corruption and a particular market's legal system strength influence the overall market expansion patterns of firms from a focal market to other foreign markets. Using the imprinting theory which suggests that firms' home market institutions become imprinted on their strategies and behaviors, and using data on international trademark registrations and institutional conditions for several emerging markets over a period of 14 years (1999–2012), the authors find corruption to be negatively associated with both the overall intensity and scope of market expansion of firms from a particular market. In addition, they discover that while the level of strength of the emerging market's legal system is negatively associated with the scope of international expansion, it is positively associated with the intensity of market expansion.

In Chapter 3, Imagawa and Nakagawa investigate how Yakult's specific marketing method — Yakult Lady method — could be an alternate market expansion strategy in emerging markets. Focusing on Yakult, a Japanese beverage maker, which developed a unique marketing method using local women in Japan in the 20th century, and now has become very successful in entering emerging markets, the authors find that Yakult method is an effective market entry strategy as it contributes to sustainable economic development. Based on an exploratory case analysis of four of Yakult's overseas businesses, they further find that the Yakult Lady method has performed well in emerging markets because it fills the institutional voids with its own resources: the well-trained Yakult Ladies. By organizing local women, Yakult develops a system that serves as a distribution network, information channel, rich pool of skilled labor and mechanism for money collection. Managers can use the findings to consider a different approach for winning in emerging markets.

In emerging markets, artificial intelligence (AI) and cyber-security play a vital role as catalysts to accelerate growth while providing mechanisms to protect and support critical infrastructure. In Chapter 4, Sarma, Matheus and Senaratne present a new pathway for growth in emerging economies via the knowledge economy and examine a critical question of what the implications are of the use and growth of AI and cyber-security in emerging economies. The authors find that the application of AI tools and techniques to specific cyber-security issues such as intelligent malware and the rapid evolution of cyber-attacks offers solutions to complex challenges faced by emerging economies. It could potentially underpin solutions for the protection of critical sectors such as education and health (cyber-security) while offering a new pathway to innovation and entrepreneurship, enabling co-operation and communication in the new knowledge economy. The authors further conceptualize the AI–cyber-security relationship in the context of economic growth and distil and connect the specific elements of AI and cyber-security that offer an advantage to emerging markets through improved output, increased income and accelerated economic performance.

Chapter 5 relates to economic performance but measures its success in terms of poverty reduction. In fact, the Joint Harmonized European Union Program of Business and Consumer Surveys produces useful data for economic modeling, forecasting and investigating poverty levels and social problems. Specifically, Čižmešija and Škrinjarić examine if the monthly data available from the consumer survey can be used to forecast future poverty rates of a country. By using the mixed sampling (MIDAS) regression analysis, the authors find that the monthly consumer data on selected variables relating to the financial situation of consumers could be used to model and forecast yearly data on the poverty rates. The implication of the findings of the chapter for policymakers of emerging markets is that they could use the MIDAS regression to forecast future poverty rates so that timely decisions can be made and action can be taken to reduce costs and increase the capacity for economic development.

In the related Chapter 6, Yang, Zhou, Chen and Carney explain what drives regional innovation capacity building in China, as building innovation capacity is critical to continuing economic development. By adopting the regional innovation system and regional innovation capacity (RIC) approaches, the authors investigate the relatively new phenomenon of RIC and identify key factors that explain variations in innovation capacity across regions of China. Their empirical results show that the key drivers of RIC differ substantively between radical innovation and incremental innovation. That is, innovation capacity is largely related to innovation inputs and these inputs tend to affect incremental innovation more than radical innovation in China. The authors contribute to literature on RIC in a transitional economic context and provide implications for future studies and government policymakers.

Innovation capacity building also relates to talent management and acquisition from the world economy. An important component of globalization over the past two decades has also been emerging markets' rapid integration into the world economy. Consequently, multinational enterprises (MNEs) have faced substantial talent management challenges to attract and retain high-performing employees. Keeping this in mind, Beamond, Farndale and Hartel in Chapter 7 address the question of how MNEs tackle these challenges by focusing on Latin America as an example of a region undergoing rapid economic development during the mining industry boom. Based on a case study of one MNE, the authors collected data through interviews in Peru, Chile and Argentina at a time of substantial skill shortages in the region. By analyzing the organizational structure of the MNE and its translation of talent management strategies from corporate to subsidiary levels, the authors explain the key actors who are in the process of translation and identify the five key talent management challenges that foreign-owned MNEs face when operating in Latin America.

Two other variables, management control systems (MCSs) and business incubators (BIs), have also been argued to support start-ups in their survival and growth. Thus, in Chapter 8, Robles and Klarner link these two variables and explain how an incubation process affect MCSs in start-ups. By using a qualitative and exploratory case study and semi-structured interviews with three start-ups and the management of the Mexican incubator *TecLean*, the authors find that an incubation process influences the development of MCSs in start-ups in at least two ways. First, an incubation process pushes the start-ups toward a non-traditional conceptualization of MCSs to include their stakeholders' perspective. Second, an incubation process highlights the relevance of MCSs when aiming at obtaining venture capital (VC) and thus increasing the start-ups' awareness and initiative to implement stricter MCSs. The implication of the study for practitioners in BIs is that they should train start-ups on the design of MCSs to increase start-ups' access to VC.

The role of the information and communication technologies (ICTs) in the creation of social networks is also important in emerging markets. To understand the importance of ICTs and the users' psychological states against these devices, Saad and Choura in Chapter 9 present their social response theoretical framework and conduct a qualitative analysis. The authors find that virtual anthropomorphic agents and commercial discussion forums with specific characteristics as main technologies can enhance the present experience on a commercial website. It is therefore essential for designers of commercial websites to use sophisticated ICTs to offer content that is sensory-based and move from a utilitarian dimension to a hedonistic one.

Singh and Camacho in Chapter 10 summarize all chapters and conclude the book.

https://doi.org/10.1142/9789811221750_0002

Chapter 2

The Impact of Home Market Institutional Conditions on Market Entry Strategies of Firms from Emerging Markets

Kelly Hewett[*,§], Alexander V. Krasnikov[†] and Adam Hepworth[‡]

[*]*University of Tennessee, Knoxville, TN 37996, USA*

[†]*Loyola University of Chicago, Chicago, IL 60660, USA*

[‡]*Ohio University, Athens, OH 45701, USA*

[§]*khewett@utk.edu*

This chapter explores how and to what extent two aspects of the regulatory institutional environment, corruption and a particular market's legal system strength, influence the overall market expansion patterns of firms from a focal market to other foreign markets. These relationships are viewed using an imprinting theory lens, which suggests that firms' home market institutions become imprinted on their strategies and behaviors. Using data on international trademark registrations and institutional conditions for several emerging markets (EMs) over a period of 14 years (1999–2012), corruption is found to be negatively associated with both the overall intensity and scope of market expansion of firms from a particular market. In addition, while the level of strength of the EM's legal system is negatively associated with the scope of international expansion, it is positively associated with the intensity of market expansion.

Introduction

Corruption is gaining increased attention in the academic literature (Birhanu *et al.*, 2015). A potential motivation for this increased interest is the generally accepted view that corruption poses a substantial risk to the viability of economic expansion in many markets (Turner, 2013). According to one appraisal, by 2020 losses caused by corruption worldwide could reach 2.5 trillion dollars annually in the construction industry alone (Machado, 2015). Those financial costs are impacting business investors' decisions as well. As a result, national governments in many countries have increased efforts to reduce corruption; they recognize that less corruption can help attract investments and level the playing field for domestic firms (Gonzalez, 2015). While corruption is a global problem, it is a particularly critical problem for emerging countries (Weitzel & Berns, 2006). Reliable legal and regulatory institutions, like the courts, are important for helping ensure enforcement of rules and agreements; they have been identified as critical factors determining market success (Latusek & Cook, 2012). Litigation provides an institutional arrangement that protects against vulnerability to the subversion of business agreements, which occurs pervasively in emerging markets (EMs) (Glaeser & Shleifer, 2003). When institutions for contract enforcement are weak, firms face greater exposure to opportunistic behavior (Khanna & Palepu, 1997) and therefore greater transaction costs (Nee, 1992).

Both corruption and the legal environment are critical factors that have been linked conceptually and empirically with firm strategy (Kaufmann & Wei, 1999). However, the relationship between the legal and regulatory environment and corruption may be more complex than some have claimed (Duvanova, 2014). Findings from some studies suggest that, counter to conventional expectations, under certain conditions corruption may occasionally benefit a firm rather than uniformly harm it. For instance, Dreher and Gassebner (2013) report that in countries characterized by high levels of bureaucracy and red tape, corruption can actually facilitate economic growth. Thus, much still needs to be understood regarding how both corruption and a country's legal environment can influence firms' strategy.

One particular outcome, foreign market expansion, has been linked to corruption as well as a country's overall legal environment (Faruq, 2011). Our study examines market expansion strategy, or the overall pattern of geographic markets to which firms from a particular country expand, and at what pace. We leverage imprinting theory (Stinchcombe, 1965) to understand these issues, focusing on firms' behaviors that are influenced by an imprint from their founding or home institutional environment (Shinkle & Kriaciunas, 2012). We also focus on EMs. As noted by Chittoor and Ray (2007, p. 338), firms from EMs competing in the global marketplace represent a trend that is "one of the distinctive phenomena of globalization in the twenty first century".

Because EM firms tend to focus on exporting as opposed to ownership as a primary mode of expansion, they continue to be intensely home-oriented (Chittoor & Ray, 2007). Thus, we expect the conditions in their home markets to be particularly relevant influences for firms' market expansion strategies. Consistent with past research, we examine the scope of the internationalization process (George *et al.*, 2005), defined as international geographic reach or the number of countries in which firms in a focal country conduct business. Moreover, we introduce an additional dimension, the intensity with which EM firms expand to foreign markets, defined as the rate at which firms in a particular category, in a particular home market expand to foreign markets (Vermeulen & Barkema, 2002). We contend that EMs' overall ineffectual regulatory institutions, characterized by weaknesses in judicial systems, poor enforcement of laws and corruption (Gani & Clemes, 2015), will exert considerable influence on firms' expansion strategies within these markets. We examine how and to what extent two aspects of the regulatory institutional environment, corruption and the nature of the legal system in a particular country, influence firms' overall market expansion patterns as they expand from a focal country to foreign markets. Through a longitudinal analysis of international trademark registration data and information on institutional conditions for 14 countries over a period of 14 years (1999–2012), we address two key questions: (1) *What is the impact of home market corruption and legal system strength on the overall intensity of international expansion of firms from EMs?* (2) *How do home market corruption and legal system strength influence the overall pattern of market expansion from EMs to other foreign markets in terms of the scope of geographic markets?*

Next, we briefly review literature relevant for our study.

Relevant Literature

According to imprinting theory (Stinchcombe, 1965), an imprint from the founding, or home, institutional environment influences firms' behaviors

(Shinkle & Kriaciunas, 2012). In EMs, these founding institutional conditions refer to conditions present before the market completely reaches developed status. The firms examined are in operation prior to such an evolution. Shinkle and Kriaciunas (2012) reveal how institutional environments, via their impacts on firms' decision blueprints, can influence competitive motivations of firms from those markets. We aim in this study to heed the call by Lounsbury and Ventresca (2002, p. 3) for more "institutionally rich studies" in research leveraging imprinting theory. Institutions are conceptualized by North (1990) as formal and informal environmental structures that govern how individuals and firms should behave within a particular context. Institutions governing firm actions are deeply rooted and differ across countries (Rodriguez *et al.*, 2005). While formal rules and laws are critically important, how regulations are implemented (Johnson *et al.*, 1998) directly influences firms. Thus, we focus specifically on the issue of laws and their observance as it pertains to the strength of the legal system in a particular country.

Academic research on institutional factors falling under the regulatory pillar has linked corruption, the strength of legal system (Luo, 2006; Rodriguez *et al.*, 2005) and regulatory intervention (Kaufmann & Wei, 1999). While some researchers view corruption as being influenced by weak institutional environments (Venard, 2009), we view corruption as part of the institutional structure; it imposes additional "rules of the game" for firms as they attempt to compete domestically as well as abroad. Empirical research focused on corruption offers evidence regarding contributing factors such as national characteristics like education and culture (Shleifer & Vishny, 1993), the level of economic freedom (Pieroni & d'Agostino, 2013) and the level of efficiency (Goudie & Stasavage, 1997).

Extant studies have also explored how corruption impacts firm-level factors such as firms' scope of internationalization (Jiménez *et al.*, 2014), market entry strategies (Rodriguez *et al.*, 2005) and behaviors in their home markets such as philanthropic behaviors and government interactions (Luo, 2006). Research on the influence of regulatory institutional factors such as legal systems and corruption largely examines these issues in host markets as opposed to home markets, and typically employs a firm-level perspective as opposed to more of an aggregate-level assessment of these phenomena. Our study is unique in its focus on the influence of home market institutional factors and in its employment of a macro-level focus on the overall pattern of movement of goods from a particular country to foreign markets. The study's longitudinal design enables us to explore changing institutional factors and their influence on local firms' market entry strategies.

Hypothesis Development

Market Expansion Strategy

Firms employing market expansion strategies seek opportunities beyond domestic markets through foreign market operations or investments. We define *market expansion strategy* as strategic expansion planning with the specific intent to enter markets outside of the home market. As our conceptual framework outlines, market expansion strategies encompass the intensity of the pace at which firms expand as well as firms' scope of expansion. Consistent with past market expansion literature, the intensity at which a firm expands (Vermeulen & Barkema, 2002) and its identified expansion markets (Barkema *et al.*, 1996) comprise the firm's diversification strategy. *Market expansion intensity* reflects the rate at which firms in a particular category from a particular home country expand to foreign markets. Greater market expansion intensity implies that firms exercise expansion strategies into more diverse product categories within foreign markets and that, in a given year, more products are targets for expansion. The *scope of market expansion* is defined as the average number of foreign markets firms target for expansion over a particular time period. Firms entering select countries gradually are said to employ market concentration strategies while rapid entry into several countries reflects a market diversification strategy (Katsikeas *et al.*, 2005) that is consistent with a broad scope of internationalization.

Research suggests that there are advantages associated with both rapid and gradual expansion strategies. While rapid market expansion can lead to new financial gains through product diversification, expansion can also burden firms with elevated distribution costs (Ayal & Zif, 1979). Gradual expansion strategies necessitate deeper market penetration at home before expanding to foreign markets (Lee & Yang, 1990; Luo & Tung, 2007). Firms vary greatly in their scope of expansion efforts. Firms with a narrow market expansion scope focus on performance maximization to attain higher profit (Ayal & Zif, 1979; Yeoh, 2004), while a narrow expansion scope can allow firms to minimize costs associated with repeat market entries. Firms with broad geographic dispersion, however, often implement international strategies to gain economies of scale advantages and capitalize on an array of knowledge acquired from operating in diverse environments (Yeoh, 2004).

Institutional Factors and Entry Strategy

Figure 1 presents our conceptual model of the impact of home country institutions on market expansion strategy. Research suggests that institutional factors play a role in determining firms' entry strategies (Chang, 1995). Specifically, characteristics of the home country institutional environment are found to influence overall performance of emerging economy firms significantly more than organizational competencies and industry factors (Gao *et al.*, 2010).

Corruption

We define corruption as "the use of public power for private benefit" (Habib & Zurawicki, 2002, p. 292). As noted, corruption comes in many forms but often results from government's weak enforcement of laws (Murtha & Lenway, 1994). Imprinted practices and decision blueprints based on firms' experiences operating in corrupt environments influence firms' strategies both inside and outside their home markets. Thus, we expect that the foundational institutional factor of corruption pervasiveness in EMs will impact both the intensity and scope of any local firm's market expansion strategies. Although corruption exists everywhere, it is

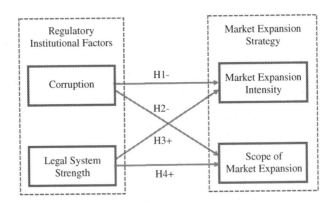

Figure 1.   Conceptual framework

oftentimes more pronounced in EMs (Rodriguez *et al.*, 2005). Historically, corruption is found to increase uncertainty (Faruq, 2011) and elevate the overall cost of doing business in a particular market (Gelbuda *et al.*, 2008). Whereas some researchers following an escapist perspective would argue that firms may indeed pursue expansion abroad in order to avoid corruption and other artifacts of weak home market regulatory institutions (Shi *et al.*, 2017), we contend that corruption will negatively impact market expansion strategies of firms. In underdeveloped institutional environments, corruption-prone officials often "customize" the level of harassment they exert on local firms such as maximizing the amount of routine kickback payments they perceive the firms are able and willing to pay (Kaufmann & Wei, 1999). Thus, firms operating in corrupt environments may be less likely to possess or acquire the necessary resources for international expansion.

Consistent with imprinting theory, as practices for dealing with corruption are imprinted on firms' practices, they become accustomed to having to rely on bribes, kickbacks, etc., simply to accomplish anything (Kaufmann *et al.*, 2003). As such, they may be less familiar with foreign markets' practices and networks and see expansion abroad as more uncertain than focusing on their home markets. In support of this reasoning, Spencer and Gomez (2011) found evidence that firms from highly institutionalized, corrupt environments faced greater obstacles and pressures when working in institutional conditions abroad.

We expect corruption to limit both the intensity and scope of market expansion. First, firms operating in corrupt institutional environments may see expansion abroad as more uncertain than continuing to focus on their home market, thereby deterring expansion and impacting intensity. Next, as the scope of expansion markets broadens, firm uncertainty increases with greater variability in low and high levels of corruption. The lack of experience in environments void of corruption will create one form of uncertainty, and the existence of corruption will introduce another form of uncertainty. We therefore expect a negative relationship between home country corruption and both intensity and scope of market expansion.

H1. *Higher levels of corruption in a home country will lead to a reduced intensity of market expansion of firms from that country.*

H2. *Higher levels of corruption in a home country will lead to a reduced scope of market expansion of firms from that country.*

Legal system strength

The *legal system strength* in a country is reflected by its power in enforcing the laws as well as the observance of its laws by members of society. A strong legal system indicates that economies have the institutional infrastructure to settle legal disputes judiciously and provide property protection (Berkowitz *et al.*, 2006). EM firms are accustomed to operating under inefficient governance systems that drive them to form relationships with market intermediaries that add to the overall costs of doing business (Khanna & Palepu, 1997); therefore, such practices will become "imprinted" on these firms' everyday routines. A weak legal system in the home market may deter firms from pursuing market expansion strategies, as operating in unfamiliar institutional environments may be risky.

Gao *et al.* (2010) find that, with a stronger home country legal institutional environment, contracts negotiated between exporters and importers can be leveraged to protect the exporter's interests (Berkowitz *et al.*, 2006), which generally reduces the uncertainty and risk of doing business abroad and may encourage both market expansion intensity and scope. With regard to intensity, a strong legal system may indirectly influence decisions to expand abroad by providing local firms with the opportunity to gain operational know-how and necessary capabilities to compete abroad. In addition, local firms may learn indirectly how to compete in other markets via their interactions with global competitors (Banerjee *et al.*, 2015). Thus, there may be additional "imprinting" of practices that will be successful against competitors operating in other markets.

As strong legal systems in the home country can facilitate market expansion, weak legal systems can stymie it. Weak home country legal systems which require local firms to seek alternative means to resolve disputes may lead to alternative practices becoming imprinted in firms' practices. In addition, insufficient contract enforcement in a firm's home market may cost the firm resources and hinder its ability to expand to other markets. To illustrate this dynamic, the Republic of Georgia's weak legal system hampered expansion efforts for a domestic mineral water company by failing to settle claims in its home market (Kuemmerle, 2012).

We expect that a strong legal system in a home market positively affects both market expansion intensity and scope. A strong legal system is expected to facilitate market expansion intensity by reducing uncertainty and lowering market expansion costs. Relative to scope of market expansion, a strong legal system ensures that firm resources are protected and provide the necessary means for market expansion. We therefore hypothesize that:

H3. *A strong home country legal system will lead to increased market expansion intensity of firms from that market.*

H4. *A strong home country legal system will lead to increased market expansion scope of firms from that market.*

Methods

Data and Sample

We leveraged data from several secondary sources. First, we extracted international trademark registration data from World Intellectual Property Organization's (WIPO) trademark registration database. WIPO prosecutes trademarks under the Madrid Agreement, simplifying the procedures for filing trademarks in different countries (Samuels & Samuels, 2004). Under this agreement, a firm may file through WIPO a single application for a trademark, which if approved, will be enforced and protected in up to 97 countries (World Intellectual Property Organization, 2016), stream-lining the protection of intellectual property (IP) rights.

We extracted trademark registrations for companies residing in the following EMs: Bulgaria, China, Croatia, Czech Republic, Egypt, Greece, Hungary, Poland, Romania, Russia, Slovakia, Slovenia, South Korea and Turkey. We extracted trademarks registered over a period of 14 years (1999–2012) during which exports from EMs grew considerably. Second, following Hallak (2006) who suggests that the level of exports may be specific to the development level of a country's particular industry/product category, we used Passport GMID to gather each country's sales information in the following categories: alcoholic drinks, apparel and footwear, beauty and personal care, consumer appliances, consumer health, fresh food, hot drinks, packaged food, retailing, soft drinks and toys and games. We used descriptions of classes of goods and services in registrations to match brands with these product categories. As such, we classified 58,991 trademark registrations, capturing approximately 87% of these countries' registrations during our time period. The merger of these databases revealed great variation between categories with respect to trademark activity. Next, we extracted information on our institutional variables from the International Country Risk Guide (ICRG) survey that reports country ratings in the three categories of risk: political, financial and economic. Finally, we used country statistics from the World Bank that capture the development of the home country's economy over the studied time period.

Measurement of Variables

Dependent variables

Our dependent variables were constructed with three considerations in mind. First, our measures capture variations in the composition of expansion not only between countries but also between product categories. Second, we are able to measure geographic scope of the expansion. Finally, our measures compare the expansion strategies over time.

We considered all three expectations in calculating both dependent variables. The first, *market expansion intensity* is the average number of trademarks registered by the companies from an emerging country j in product category i during year t. Such a granular measure accounts for variations between different product categories. The second dependent variable, *scope of expansion strategy*, is the average number of countries per international trademark application filed by companies from emerging country j in product category i during year t. In summary, we obtained 2,156 observations for 14 countries, 11 product categories and 14 years (1999–2012).

Independent variables

We use two indicators of our predictors, *Corruption* and *Law and Order*, derived from the ICRG, published by PRS group. *Corruption* reflects "the use of public power for private benefit" (Habib & Zurawicki, 2002, p. 292) and is typically manifested in behaviors such as the prevalence of practices where the government or other actors demand special payments or bribes (Howell, 2014). Our second indicator, *law and order*, measures the strength of the legal system and observance of law, which is important for business because it captures mechanisms for adjudicating disputes and enforcing property and contractual rights (Howell, 2014).

Control variables

We used two variables from the ICRG survey, *investment profile* and *socioeconomic conditions*, to control for home country conditions that may (de)emphasize firms' expansion. While the former reflects contract enforcement, payment delays and the ability to retain profits, the latter is related to overall economic pressures such as poverty and unemployment (Howell, 2014). Countries with higher levels of socioeconomic conditions were characterized by lower poverty and higher consumer confidence. Overall, markets with higher scores on these two dimensions are characterized by lower institutional risks. We also used *GDP per capita* (in thousands of dollars) because it could affect firms' expansion decisions. This measure was derived from the World Bank. Finally, *category size* is measured as total sales in the respective category in the respective domestic market (in millions of dollars).

Model

Variable descriptive statistics and correlations are presented in Table 1. Since our sample has a nested structure, which may result in heteroscedasticity of errors (White, 1980), we estimated a maximum likelihood regression model with fixed country, category and time effects. To exploit the panel nature of our data and account for potential endogeneity, we

Table 1. Descriptive statistics ($N = 2,156$)[a]

Variable	Mean	St.D.	1	2	3	4	5	6	7
1. Market expansion intensity	18.55	31.29	1.00						
2. Scope of market expansion	12.45	7.66	−0.01	1.00					
3. Corruption	2.80	0.88	−0.19	−0.01	1.00				
4. Legal system strength	4.35	0.74	−0.02	−0.09	0.53	1.00			
5. Socioeconomic conditions	5.84	1.55	0.12	−0.26	−0.02	0.22	1.00		
6. Investment profile	8.97	2.16	0.05	−0.18	−0.29	−0.16	0.31	1.00	
7. GDP per capita (in thousands of dollars)	9.91	6.98	0.05	−0.29	−0.10	0.11	0.58	0.58	1.00
8. Category size (in millions of dollars)	23.18	98.10	0.10	−0.02	−0.15	0.01	0.14	−0.22	−0.12

Note: [a]All correlations with absolute values >0.05 are significantly different from 0 at $p < 0.05$.

included the lagged dependent variables in the respective equations (Chang & Wu, 2014). As such, our model is as follows:

$$\begin{aligned} DV_{ij(t+1)} = f(&DV_{ijt}, Corruption_{ijt}, Legal\ System\ Strength_{ijt}, \\ &Socioeconomic\ Conditions_{ijt}, Investment\ Profile_{ijt}, \\ &GDP\ per\ Capita_{ijt}, Category\ Size_{ijt}, Country \\ &Fixed\ Effects_i, Product\ Category\ Fixed\ Effects_j, \\ &Time\ Fixed\ Effects_t), \end{aligned} \quad (1)$$

where DV is either intensity or the scope of a firm's expansion strategy.

Results

Table 2 displays the results of the ML fixed effect regression models predicting *market expansion intensity* using the full sample of country–product category–time observations. Model 1a includes a lagged dependent variable, *corruption*, as the predictor and all control variables; while in Model 2a *legal system strength* is used as the predictor. Finally, Model 3a includes the full set of variables and controls. The results lend support to the hypothesis that corruption negatively affects expansion

Table 2. Parameter estimates (standard errors) of the ML regression with country, year and category fixed effects

	Independent variables	Model 1a	Model 2a	Model 3a
	Intercept	0.89(0.13)**	0.65(0.17)**	0.64(0.17)**
1	Lagged market expansion intensity	0.78(0.01)**	0.78(0.01)**	0.78(0.01)**
2	Corruption	–0.04(0.02)*	—	–0.08(0.03)*
3	Legal system strength	—	0.04(0.02)*	0.08(0.03)*
4	Socioeconomic conditions	–0.02(0.02)	–0.02(0.02)	–0.02(0.02)
5	Investment profile	–0.01(0.01)	–0.01(0.01)	–0.01(0.01)
6	GDP per capita	0.00(0.00)	0.00(0.00)	0.00(0.00)
7	Category size	0.00(0.00)	0.00(0.00)	0.00(0.00)
	R^2	0.64	0.63	0.68
	F-statistics	553.77	551.50	576.20
	p-value	<0.01	<0.01	<0.01
	N	2,156.00	2,156.00	2,156.00

Note: Dependent variable — market expansion intensity. * $p < 0.05$, ** $p < 0.01$.

strategies as measured by intensity (H1). Moreover, the inclusion of the both predictors in Model 3a did not change the direction or significance of the estimated slopes for the predictors and control variables. Specifically, parameter estimates for *corruption* in both Models 1a and 3a were negative and significantly different from 0 ($\beta = -0.043$, $p < 0.05$ and $\beta = -0.080$, $p < 0.05$, respectively). Hypothesis 3 was also supported, suggesting that strong legal systems support international expansion intensity (in Model 2a, $\beta = 0.041$, $p < 0.05$, and in Model 3a, $\beta = 0.081$, $p < 0.05$). None of the control variables were significant. The overall model fit (R-squared) varied from 0.63 (Model 2a) to 0.68 (Model 3a) suggesting that the full model provides better fit and results are not driven by mere correlations between institutional predictors.

Table 3 provides results regarding the impact of corruption and legal system strength on the *scope of international expansion.* Overall fit of Models 1b, 2b and 3b varied between 0.14 and 0.18 with the highest R^2 corresponding to the full model. Similar to the previous analyses, *corruption* had a negative impact both in the reduced Model 1b ($\beta = -0.874$, $p < 0.001$) and full Model 3b ($\beta = -0.616$, $p < 0.05$). That is, higher corruption in home countries reduces the geographic scope of expansion

Table 3. Parameter estimates (standard errors) of the ML regression with country, year and category fixed effects

	Independent variables	Model 1b	Model 2b	Model 3b
	Intercept	15.09(1.20)**	17.15(1.54)**	17.11(1.53)**
1	Lagged scope of market expansion	0.19(0.02)**	0.20(0.02)**	0.19(0.02)**
2	Corruption	−0.87(0.24)**	—	−0.62(−0.23)*
3	Legal system strength	—	−0.91(0.25)**	−0.60(0.29)*
4	Socioeconomic conditions	−0.59(0.12)**	−0.53(0.13)**	−0.55(0.13)**
5	Investment profile	0.25(0.11)*	0.15(0.11)	0.21(0.11)*
6	GDP-per-capita	−0.19(0.03)**	−0.17(0.03)**	−0.17(0.03)**
7	Category size	−0.00(0.00)	−0.00(0.00)	−0.00(0.00)
	R^2	0.16	0.14	0.18
	F-statistics	61.06	57.46	63.07
	p-value	<0.01	<0.01	<0.01
	N	2,156.00	2,156.00	2,156.00

Note: Dependent variable — scope of market expansion. * $p < 0.05$, ** $p < 0.01$.

strategies of the firms from those countries. Next, contrary to H4, *legal system strength* negatively impacts the scope of international expansion in both Models 2b and 3b ($\beta = -0.906$, $p < 0.001$ and $\beta = -0.603$, $p < 0.05$, respectively). That is, stronger observance of laws inhibits the international scope of EM firms. Among our controls, *socioeconomic conditions* has the strongest negative impact on the scope of international expansion ($\beta = -0.550$, $p < 0.001$ in Model 3), suggesting that firms in countries with lower social pressures are more likely to focus on serving their own populations rather than expanding to other markets. Next, the estimate for *investment profile* was positive and significant in Models 1b ($\beta = 0.251$, $p < 0.05$) and 3b ($\beta = 0.205$, $p < 0.05$) but not in Model 2b ($\beta = 0.151$, $p = 0.15$). Nevertheless, our results provide further evidence that countries with attractive investment climates may facilitate domestic firms' expansion.

Robustness Analysis

A battery of robustness checks resulted in the same pattern of support for the hypothesized effects of institutional forces on international expansion strategies. First, we excluded two control variables (*socioeconomic conditions* and *investment profile*) to reduce correlations between predictors and reduce the bias associated with predictors and controls coming from the same source. The hypothesized relationships do not change; however, the explanatory power of the model significantly drops. Next, we tried to address the nested structure of our data by running a hierarchical linear model (Raudenbush & Bryk, 2002). The direction or statistical significance of the hypothesized tests do not change. As such, we report results of the more parsimonious analysis. Finally, we added other institutional variables from ICRG; however, the model begins to suffer from increasing multicollinearity, so we use the model in Equation (1).

Discussion

In this study, we sought to address two primary research questions.

Research question #1: *What is the impact of home market institutional conditions on the overall intensity of international expansion of firms from EMs?*

Our findings support the notion that less developed institutional environments in EMs can negatively impact the overall intensity of international expansion by firms in those markets. In particular, high levels of corruption and less developed legal and judicial systems can reduce firms' abilities and/or willingness to embark on an intensive strategy for global expansion. As opposed to arguments that weak regulatory environments may actually benefit EM firms as they develop coping mechanisms that can be leveraged in uncertain destination markets (Hansen *et al.*, 2018; Marano *et al.*, 2016), we find that, as weak legal and judicial systems create uncertainty in firms' home markets, these firms often enforce contracts informally via local networks (Taussig & Delios, 2014) and are less likely to expand abroad. We find that, when markets are high in corruption and the strength and impartiality of the legal systems are low, the overall level of trademark applications from those countries is lower.

Research question #2: *How do institutional conditions influence the overall pattern of market expansion from EMs to other foreign markets in terms of the scope of geographic markets?*

Our findings demonstrate mixed results in terms of how less developed institutional environments impact EM firms' scope of expansion. First, we find that firms from more corrupt home markets submit applications to register their trademarks in fewer countries than firms from less corrupt home markets. However, stronger and more impartial legal systems also appear to impede the overall scope of firms' geographic expansion. While this finding may seem counterintuitive, we found evidence in the marketing literature that weaker legal environments may actually support broader market expansion. Specifically, Luo and Tung (2007) contend that a weak legal environment of a home country (notably the insufficient law enforcement and substandard property protection rights) restrains competitiveness within those markets and may push domestic firms to internationalize to transparent, efficient legal systems. In addition, there is evidence that liabilities such as "outsidership" and low market knowledge are central issues for firms when attempting to grow in new markets (Vahlne & Johanson 2017) and may impact firms less as they intensify efforts in markets they have already entered.

Implications

Our primary theoretical contribution is found in the impacts that corruption and law and order exert on firm's market expansion strategies. Institutional theory suggests that business performance requires reliable institutions that ensure rules and agreements are enforced (Latusek & Cook, 2012). While we find a negative impact of corruption and positive impact of the strength of legal system on the intensity of firms' expansion efforts, our results indicate that both these factors reduce the scope of geographic expansion. As such, the impact of regulatory institutional factors is complex. One aspect studied here, corruption, appears to consistently hinder firms in both the intensity and scope of their market expansion activities. The strength of legal system aids in an intensive market expansion strategy yet appears to decrease the scope of expansion. That finding is consistent with prior research (Luo & Tung, 2007) demonstrating that scope of expansion may be related to firms' efforts to overcome institutional constraints at home. These results illuminate the complex nature of the institutional environment on EM firm expansion strategies.

Our results indicate that home country corruption and a weak legal system may deter firms from intensive international expansion. Alena Akhmadullina, owner of one of the most successful Russian fashion brands, recognized that focused exporting decisions as opposed to intensive expansion are largely driven by regulatory inefficiencies in the Russian market (Vedomosti, 2015). Therefore, firms are limited in their ability to dedicate attention and resources abroad due to the demands in its home market.

EM firms may consider more expansion opportunities when the domestic legal system does not offer adequate laws and contract enforcement. In such cases, outward-looking firms may attempt to reduce their overall costs associated with bribery or other factors related to corruption and alternative modes of contract enforcement by pursuing intensive internationalization. Finally, our results also suggest that greater legal protection may increase the attractiveness of markets not only for investors but also for domestic firms. Thus, there may be a decrease in firms' motivations to pursue expansion to a wide range of markets as the legal system evolves in a particular market.

Aside from offering potential direction for global managers, our results also have interesting implications for governments and policymakers. First, as many EMs have introduced pro-market regulatory reforms that lift barriers to starting businesses and transferring property (World Bank 2019), our results would offer reassurance that these efforts may positively influence domestic firms' expansion. In particular, our results suggest that investing in regulatory reforms that reduce corruption and result in greater legal protections for intellectual property such as brands may encourage domestic firms to dedicate resources to and subsequently seek to appropriate value from their brand assets (Han *et al.*, 2017) by expanding abroad. Because the intensity of expansion as opposed to scope of destination markets will be primary in terms of impacting a country's balance of trade, the contrary impact of such reforms on the scope of expansion should be of less concern to policymakers.

Limitations

As with any research of this scope, this study is not without limitations. First, due to significant challenges with compiling such a rich dataset, our sample is unavoidably limited in scope and our analyses reveal average effects. Future research should attempt to examine similar relationships not only using a larger number of firms but also a greater number of industries and countries. Next, characteristics of individual EM firms' brand strategies (e.g. positioning, marketing mix elements) could influence EM brand expansion decisions and performance in destination markets. Future research should explore such variables' influence on relationships such as those examined here, potentially taking into consideration individual brand- or firm-level variables. Finally, whereas the focus in our study was on regulatory conditions in EM firms' home markets, EM institutional reform has been argued to be dynamic and multidimensional (Ault and Spicer, 2014), e.g. comprising changes in other aspects of a market's institutional environment. Thus, future studies might also incorporate informal institutions and seek to understand how the mix of formal and informal institutions affects the transaction costs for firms pursuing expansion.

References

Ault, J. & Spicer, A. (2014). The institutional context of poverty: state fragility as a predictor of cross-national variation in commercial microfinance lending. *Strategic Management Journal*, 35(12), 1818–1838.

Ayal, I. & Zif, J. (1979). Market expansion strategies in multinational marketing. *Journal of Marketing*, 43(2), 84–94.

Banerjee, S., Prabhu, J.C. & Chandy, R.K. (2015). Indirect learning: How emerging-market firms grow. *Journal of Marketing*, 79(1), 10–28.

Barkema, H., Bell, J. & Pennings, J. (1996). Foreign entry, cultural barriers and learning. *Strategic Management Journal*, 17(2), 151–166.

Berkowitz, D., Moenius, J. & Pistor, K. (2006). Trade, law, and product complexity. *The Review of Economics and Statistics*, 88(2), 363–373.

Birhanu, A.G., Gambardella, A. & Valentini, G. (2015). Bribery and investment: firm-level evidence from Africa and Latin America. *Strategic Management Journal*, 37(9), 1865–1877.

Chang, S.J. (1995). International expansion strategy of Japanese firms: capability building through sequential entry. *Academy of Management Journal*, 38(2), 383–407.

Chang, S.J. & Wu, B. (2014). Institutional barriers and industry dynamics. Strategic *Management Journal*, 35(8), 1103–1123.

Chittoor, R. & Ray, S. (2007). Internationalization paths of Indian pharmaceutical firms — a strategic group analysis. *Journal of International Management*, 13(3), 338–355.

Dreher, A. & Gassebner, M. (2013). Greasing the wheels? The impact of regulations and corruption on firm entry. *Public Choice*, 155(3–4), 413–432.

Duvanova, D. (2014). Economic regulations, red tape, and bureaucratic corruption in post-communist economies. *World Development*, 59, 298–312.

Faruq, H.A. (2011). How institutions affect export quality. *Economic Systems*, 35(4), 586–606.

Gani, A. & Clemes, M.D. (2015). Natural resource exports and corruption. *International Advances in Economic Research*, 21(2), 239–240.

Gao, G.Y., Murray, J.Y., Kotabe, M. & Lu, J. (2010). A "strategy tripod" perspective on export behaviors: evidence from domestic and foreign firms based in an emerging economy. *Journal of International Business Studies*, 41(3), 377–396.

Gelbuda, M., Meyer, K.E. & Delios, A. (2008). International business and institutional development in Central and Eastern Europe. *Journal of International Management*, 14(1), 1–11.

George, G., Wiklund, J. & Zahra, S.A. (2005). Ownership and the internationalization of small firms. *Journal of Management*, 31(2), 210–233.

Glaeser E. & Shleifer A. (2003). The rise of the regulatory state. *Journal of Economic Literature*, 41(2), 401–425.

Gonzalez, D. (2015). 5 steps for managing corruption risk in Mexico. *Forbes*. Retrieved from: https://www.forbes.com/sites/riskmap/2015/10/22/5-steps-for-managing-corruption-risk-in-mexico [Accessed on August 8, 2019].

Goudie, A.W. & Stasavage, D. (1997). Corruption: The issues.: Organisation for Economic Co-Operation and Development, Paris.

Habib, M. & Zurawicki, L. (2002). Corruption and foreign direct investment. *Journal of International Business Studies*, 33(2), 291–307.

Hallak, J.C. (2006). Product quality and the direction of trade. *Journal of International Economics*, 68(1), 238–265.

Han, K., Mittal, V. & Zhang, Y. (2017). Relative strategic emphasis and firm-idiosyncratic risk: the moderating role of relative performance and demand instability. *Journal of Marketing*, 81(4), 25–44.

Hansen, M.W., Langevang, T., Rutashobya, L. & Urassa, G. (2018). Coping with the African business environment: enterprise strategy in response to institutional uncertainty in Tanzania. *Journal of African Business*, 19(1), 1–26.

Howell, L.D. (2014). Evaluating political risk forecasting models: what works? *Thunderbird International Business Review*, 56(4), 305–316.

Jiménez, A., Luis-Rico, I. & Benito-Osorio, D. (2014). The influence of political risk on the scope of internationalization of regulated companies: insights from a Spanish sample. *Journal of World Business*, 49(3), 301–311.

Johnson, S., Kaufmann, D. & Zoido-Lobatón, P. (1998). Regulatory discretion and the unofficial economy. *American Economic Review*, 88(2), 387–392.

Katsikeas, E.S., Papavassiliou, N., Theodosiou, M. & Morgan, R.E. (2005). Export market expansion strategies of direct-selling small and medium-sized firms: implications for export sales management activities. *Journal of International Marketing*, 13(2), 57–92.

Kaufmann, D. & Wei, S.J. (1999). Does "grease money" speed up the wheels of commerce?: National Bureau of Economic Research.

Kaufmann, D., Kraay, A. & Mastruzzi, M. (2003). Governance matters III: governance indicators for 1996, 1998, 2000, and 2002. *The World Bank Economic Review*, 18(2), 253–287.

Khanna, T. & Palepu, K. (1997). Why focused strategies may be wrong for emerging markets. *Harvard Business Review*, 75(4), 41–54.

Kuemmerle, W. (2012). The entrepreneur's path to global expansion. *MIT Sloan Management Review*, 46(2), 42-49.

Latusek, D. & Cook, K.S. (2012). Trust in transitions. *Kyklos*, 65(4), 512–525.

Lee, C.S. & Yang, Y.S. (1990). Impact of export market expansion strategy on export performance. *International Marketing Review*, 7(4), 41–51.

Lounsbury, M. & Ventresca, M.J. (2002). *Social Structure and Organizations Revisited.* Amsterdam, The Netherlands: Emerald Group Publishing Limited, pp. 3–36.

Luo, Y. (2006). Political behavior, social responsibility, and perceived corruption: a structuration perspective. *Journal of International Business Studies*, 37(6), 747–766.

Luo, Y. & Tung, R.L. (2007). International expansion of emerging market enterprises: a springboard perspective. *Journal of International Business Studies*, 38(4), 481–498.

Machado, A. (2015). Corruption and monopolies — An endemic problem. *Forbes*, Retrieved from: https://www.forbes.com/sites/arthurmachado/2015/07/20/corruption-and-monopolies/ [Accessed on August 12, 2019].

Marano, V., Arregle, J.-L., Hitt, M.A., Spadafora, E. & van Essen, M. (2016). Home country institutions and the internationalization-performance relationship: a meta-analytic review. *Journal of Management*, 42(5), 1075–1110.

Murtha, T.P. & Lenway, S.A. (1994). Country capabilities and the strategic state: how national political institutions affect multinational corporations' strategies. *Strategic Management Journal*, 15(S2) 113–129.

Nee, V. (1992). Organizational dynamics of market transition: hybrid forms, property rights, and mixed economy in China. *Administrative Science Quarterly*, 37(1), 1–27.

North, D.C. (1990). *Institutions, Instutional Change and Economic Performance: Political Economy of Institutions and Decisions*. Cambridge, UK: Cambridge University Press.

Pieroni, L. & d'Agostino, G. (2013). Corruption and the effects of economic freedom. *European Journal of Political Economy*, 29, 54–72.

Raudenbush, S.W. & Bryk, A.S. (2002). *Hierarchical Linear Models: Applications and Data Analysis Methods*. Thousand Oaks, CA: Sage.

Robertson, C.J. & Watson, A. (2004). Corruption and change: the impact of foreign direct investment. *Strategic Management Journal*, 25(4), 385–396.

Rodriguez, P., Uhlenbruck, K. & Eden, L. (2005). Government corruption and the entry strategies of multinationals. *Academy of Management Review*, 30(2), 383–396.

Samuels, J.M. & Samuels, L.B. (2004). International trademark prosecution streamlined: the Madrid Protocol comes into force in the United States. *Journal Intellectual Property Law*, 12, 151–161.

Shi, W., Sun, S.L., Yan, D. & Zhu, Z. (2017). Institutional fragility and outward foreign direct investment from China. *Journal of International Business Studies*, 48(4), 452–476.

Shinkle, G.A. &. Kriauciunas, A.P. (2002). The impact of current and founding institutions on strength of competitive aspirations in transition economies. *Strategic Management Journal*, 33(4), 448–458.

Shleifer, A. & Vishny, R.W. (1993). Corruption. *The Quarterly Journal of Economics*, 108(3): 599–617.

Spencer, J. & Gomez, C. (2011). MNEs and corruption: the impact of national institutions and subsidiary strategy. *Strategic Management Journal*, 32(3), 280–300.

Stinchcombe, A.L. (1965). Social structure and organizations. In J.G. March (ed.), *Handbook of organizations*. Chicago: Rand McNally, pp. 142–193.

Taussig, M. & Delios, A. (2014). Unbundling the effects of institutions on firm resources: the contingent value of being local in emerging economy private equity. *Strategic Management Journal*, 36(12), 1845–1865.

Treisman, D. (2000). The causes of corruption: a cross-national study. *Journal of Public Economics*, 76(3), 399–457.

Turner, M. (2013). Corruption poses largest threat to emerging markets in ECR survey. Euromoney, Retrieved from: https://www.euromoney.com/article/b12kjtls6wjxzz/corruption-poses-largest-threat-to-emerging-markets-in-ecr-survey [Accessed on July 14, 2019].

Vahlne, J.E. & Johanson, J. (2017). From internationalization to evolution: the Uppsala model at 40 years., 48(9), 1087–1102.

Vedomosti (2015). Interview with Alina Alkhmadullin. Retrived from: http://www.vedomosti.ru/lifestyle/characters/2015/12/14/620476-ya-poka-na-vseh-grablyah-ne-postoyala-uroki-ne-viuchila#/galleries/140737492553920/normal/2 [Accessed on January 7, 2016].

Venard, B. (2009). Organizational isomorphism and corruption: an empirical research in Russia. *Journal of Business Ethics*, 89(1), 59–76.

Vermeulen, F. & Barkema, H. (2002). Pace, rhythm, and scope: process dependence in building a profitable multinational corporation. *Strategic Management Journal*, 23(7), 637–653.

Weitzel, U. & Berns, S. (2006). Cross-border takeovers, corruption, and related aspects of governance. *Journal of International Business Studies*, 37(6), 786–806.

White, H. (1980). A heteroskedasticity-consistent covariance matrix estimator and a direct test for heteroskedasticity. *Econometrica: Journal of the Econometric Society*, 48(4), 817–838.

World Bank (2019). *Doing Business 2019.* Washington, DC: World Bank Group.

World Intellectual Property Organization. (2016). Madrid System. Retrieved from: http://www.wipo.int/madrid/en/ [Accessed on January 5, 2016].

Yeoh, P.L. (2004). International learning: antecedents and performance implications among newly internationalizing companies in an exporting context. *International Marketing Review*, 21(4/5), 511–535.

Chapter 3

Women Who Fill the Institutional Voids: Why has the Yakult Lady Method Succeeded in Emerging Markets?

Tomomi Imagawa* and Koichi Nakagawa

Osaka University, Suita, Osaka 565-0871, Japan

tomomi.imagawa@gmail.com

This chapter investigates why Yakult's specific marketing method, the "Yakult Lady method", has been effective to enter emerging markets. Yakult, a Japanese beverage maker, developed a unique marketing method using local women in Japan in the 20th century. Now, it has become Yakult's key success factor in its overseas businesses, especially in emerging markets. It has also been considered a good way of doing business in emerging countries because it contributes to sustainable economic development. However, scholars know little about why it has succeeded in emerging markets from a business competitiveness perspective. Based on an exploratory case analysis of four of Yakult's overseas businesses, we find that the Yakult Lady method has performed well in emerging markets because it filled the institutional voids with its own resources — the well-trained Yakult Ladies. By organizing local women, Yakult develops a system that serves as a distribution network, information channel, rich pool of skilled labor and mechanism for money collection. Such findings present a different approach from previous studies for winning in emerging markets.

Introduction

From the perspective of the theory of institutional voids, this chapter examines the reasons why the Yakult's unique sales method, the *Yakult Lady method*, has achieved sustainable success in emerging markets. Yakult, a global healthy beverage company headquartered in Japan, established its own sales method after the Second World War and has been very successful in emerging markets. As shown in Figure 1, it has acquired substantial market share in more than 10 countries (Goyaland & Gupta, 2015; Sugawara, 2010). In recent years, Yakult and its approach have attracted considerable attention as an ideal method of conducting business in emerging countries, especially with those at the base of the pyramid (BOP) (Mathur *et al.*, 2016), where it is considered a desirable approach to sustainable development that makes local people commit to the business (Prahalad, 2006). Additionally, by providing employment opportunities to local women, the Yakult Lady method is considered to be well in line with the BOP business philosophy (Mizuo, 2016). Learning from the Yakult Lady method, companies such as Grameen Danone and Hindustan Unilever have similarly launched their BOP businesses (Ghalib *et al.*, 2009; Raja & Arunachalam, 2011).

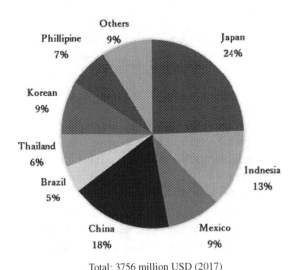

Total: 3756 million USD (2017)

Figure 1.   Product sales volume ratio by country (2017)

Source: Yakult Honsha Website.

Despite the considerable attention this method has received, one major question remains: Why has the Yakult Lady method succeeded in seizing significant market share? While most studies have explained the Yakult Lady method and its significance for sustainable economic development, few studies have investigated its competitive advantages. Therefore, this study intends to analyze how Yakult cultivated the emerging market using the theory of institutional voids (Khanna & Palepu, 2010). In terms of academic contributions, from the case of Yakult, this study intends to advance the study of strategies that function well under environments characterized by several institutional voids. Institutional voids, an application of the institutionalism theory to emerging markets, have been regarded one of the central theoretical frameworks that describe the economic features of emerging markets. However, there are not many studies regarding how to do business successfully under such a variety of voids. In this sense, this study will take a step toward further understanding business in emerging markets — how business entities can fill the institutional voids.

Literature Review

The Mechanism of the Yakult Lady Method

The Yakult Lady method is a mechanism by which a healthy, functional beverage named "Yakult" (the same as the company name) is sold by local women as sales agents (Nakagawa & Imagawa, 2019; Sugawara, 2010). The company offers an on-the-job training program that enables beginners to become fully skilled sales representatives. The first distinctive characteristic of the Yakult Lady method is the contracting of local women as self-employed sales agents and paying them according to their sales performance, not as a fixed salary. At first glance, it seems to be a difficult method for Yakult ladies. However, since the women become independent business owners working under a piece-rate wage system after being taught the sales method, they become highly motivated and they are usually able to earn a higher income than those working in other jobs in their respective countries. This type of employment style is considered to be in line with the philosophy of BOP business (Prahalad, 2006).

The Yakult Group has entered into contracts with thousands of such local women (mainly housewives) in most emerging markets, covering almost all areas in the countries in which it operates and thus contributing both to Yakult's business development and that of the local societies (Nakagawa & Imagawa, 2019). On the one hand, the Yakult Group can reach all customers by contracting local housewives as sales agents because they have close relationships with their local communities (Sugawara, 2010). On the other hand, this method provides employment opportunities to women who often face difficulties in getting jobs that can provide good income. Thus, the Yakult Lady method has been recognized as one of the ideal business models at the BOP, with many other players imitating its approach, such as Grameen Danone (Raja & Arunachalam, 2011; Sugawara 2010).

The other important characteristic of the Yakult Lady method is following an on-the-spot, face-to-face, cash-only sales approach. When an agent sells the product, she visits the customer's home and tries to sell the beverage for cash (Figure 2). The agent explains the healthy functions of the product in detail to convince the customer that the product serves his/her family's needs (Goyaland & Gupta, 2015; Nakagawa & Imagawa, 2019).

Afterward, the Yakult Lady submits the sales proceeds to the company after one business day and receives her payment at the end of the month. Therefore, the income generated by working for Yakult always surpasses the work expenses, thus alleviating poverty. However, while

Figure 2. An Image illustrating the process of selling products at the customer's home

Source: Yakult Honsha Website.

Yakult places great importance on the Yakult Lady method, it also uses retail stores as a supplementary sales channel. Although the Yakult Lady method has an advantage in attracting customers in rural communities, it is not effective in urban areas. Therefore, Yakult uses both the Yakult Lady method and retail stores to build an efficient distribution system in each country (Nakagawa & Imagawa, 2019).

The History of the Yakult Lady Method

The prototype of the Yakult Lady method is a unique marketing/sales method called *Eigyo* that was developed in postwar Japan (Johansson & Nonaka, 1996). While the sales force in European and American companies is only responsible for the implementation of the marketing strategy developed by the headquarters, in Japanese companies, the sales force both develops and executes the strategy. To make this possible, Japanese companies allocate the business elites to the Eigyo departments, train them intensively and empower them to make decisions. This approach is quite effective in acquiring market share because the sales personnel can develop good relationships with their counterparts for collecting useful information from customers and responding to changes occurring in the market.

Based on the Japanese Eigyo marketing method, Yakult launched its original sales method in Japan in 1963 and continued to improve upon it throughout the 1960s. According to the Yakult Lady method, the company must contract with women living in local areas where they have close relationships, since they can easily start selling the product using their existing social networks. Further, they work as a franchised Yakult Lady, who is an independent, self-employed person. Although the primary goal is to reduce the company's employment costs, it also provides a strong incentive for women to work hard for themselves, while maintaining their free time for housekeeping (Sugawara, 2010). After completing the development of the Yakult Lady method in the 1960s, Yakult started expanding its business into several emerging markets, such as Taiwan, Brazil and Hong Kong. Their tremendous success encouraged them to expand to more than 10 countries, which are mostly categorized as emerging markets. At present, Yakult is considered one of the most successful Japanese companies operating in emerging markets (Goyaland & Gupta, 2015; Horn, 2009).

Yakult has attracted global attention due to its high compatibility with the BOP business philosophy (Prahalad, 2006). As a means of sustainable development that complements aid and donations, BOP business emphasizes the importance of incentives to local people. By establishing a system that converts local people into business co-developers and minimizes the risks they undertake, a company that tries to do business at the BOP can establish strong business operations. This approach motivates the local employees and partners to behave in a manner that seeks to maximize their own economic return. In addition, with a high motivation to succeed, local people try to obtain business skills, thus making sustainable development of the local area more likely (London & Hart, 2004; Prahalad, 2006). These features of an ideal BOP business method strongly correspond to those of the Yakult Lady method, which provides employment opportunities to women who are often socially vulnerable, helps them to learn management skills and gain economic independence and contributes to improving the overall health of people living in areas with poor sanitary levels through the provision of healthy beverages. Since the Yakult Lady method proved to be effective, other followers have emerged utilizing the same method, such as the *Danone lady* by Grameen Danone, *Shakti* of Hindustan Unilever and the *Polygul lady* of Japan Polygul (Jacob & Kwok, 2011; Rangan & Rajan, 2007; Sugawara, 2010).

Comparison with the Similar Sales Method

To clarify the characteristics of Yakult Lady method, in this section, we compare it to similar sales methods: Japanese Eigyo (Johansson & Nonaka, 1996) and the Western approach to person-to-person relationship sales adopted by Omnilife and Amway (Cahn, 2006; Pratt, 2000). Like the Yakult Lady Method, Omnilife and Amway expand their sales channels using individual agents instead of their own employees or distribution companies. However, in the case of these companies, the purpose is different. The Yakult Lady method leaves the business to individual agents in order to overcome the shortage of distribution infrastructure and does not seek to take advantage of the women's personal relationships; Yakult agents try to find new customers there. On the contrary, Omnilife and Amway actively aim to exploit sales agents' personal relationships: family, friends and neighborhoods. While the Yakult Lady method relies on trust for the agents' success, it is the trust that the agents have gained through their attitude toward working for customers, not their existing personal relationships. In contrast, Omnilife and Amway's sales depend on the agents' personal trustworthiness based on their past interactions with colleagues. In summary, the Western style of person-to-person sales relies on personal relationships, while the Yakult Lady Method is one that does not depend on personal connections and starts developing sales channels from scratch.

The Yakult Lady method was established based on the concept of providing employment to women and promoting self-reliance. Therefore, it provides effective training and a generous support system for agents so that they can achieve sufficient benefits. As a result, most agents earn enough to make a living from their sales activities. Omnilife, for example, considers the sales activities of individual agents as goodwill-based charitable activities, as symbolized by its slogan — *People helping people*. In fact, opportunities for individual agents to develop sales skills are not sufficient, and only a few people can make a living with the rewards they get from Omnilife. In the Western style of person-to-person sales, only companies are able to generate sufficient profits. In contrast, the Yakult Lady method benefits both Yakult and the individual agents through their successful sales efforts.

Table 1 summarizes the differences between the three approaches and the following is a summary of the features of the Yakult Lady method compared to the Japanese "Eigyo". The major difference between the Yakult Lady Method and "Eigyo" is the type of contract between the company and the salesperson. While "Eigyo" leaves sales to employees, the Yakult Lady method relies on individual agents. As individual agents get paid on a piece-by-piece basis, the Yakult Lady method makes sales incentives even greater. The other characteristics are almost the same. Both expect a salesperson to build a trusting relationship with the customer and bring stable sales to the company. In short, the lady method is a system that strengthens the incentive system by converting the "Eigyo" salesperson into an individual agent.

Research Gap

However, it can be pointed out that there is still an academic gap in understanding the competitive rationale for person-to-person sales methods in emerging markets. Although it is claimed that the Yakult Lady and similar sales methods are in line with the idea of developing a healthy economy through business (Leliveld & Knorringa, 2018; Rangan & Rajan, 2007; Sugawara, 2010), it is not clear why the mechanism has been effective in capturing considerable share in local markets and building economically

Table 1.   **Comparison of companies using person-to-person sales**

	Yakult	**Omnilife, Amway**	**Japanese Eigyo**
Entity responsible for sales	Individual agent	Individual agent	Own employees
Reason for leaving the business to an external entity	To overcome institutional voids (defective logistics and transportation infrastructure)	To use the individual agent's social capital	
Reason for company-led sales activity	To build stable relationships with customers' buyers and earn stable sales		To build stable relationships with customers' buyers and earn stable sales
Positioning of sales activities	Economic activity	Charity	Economic activity
Remuneration for sales activities	Sufficient for living	Most cannot make a living	Sufficient for living
Purpose of sales training	Improve knowledge and sales skills	Sales motivation	Improve knowledge and sales skills

sustainable businesses. No matter how much social impact a business model generates, if it is not economically sustainable, it cannot continue. In this sense, the success of the Yakult Lady Method and similar person-to-person sales approaches may be due to the fact that these systems are competitively advantageous in emerging markets. However, few studies have investigated these systems in terms of competitive rationality. In order to answer the research question, it would be effective to use a framework that can clarify the characteristics of emerging markets, explore the case inductively and answer why person-to-person sales work well under those characteristics. Thus, this study analyzes why the Yakult Lady method has been effective in emerging markets, using the theoretical framework of institutional voids.

Analytical Framework: The Institutional Voids

The institutional voids perspective is considered one of the well-developed concepts for understanding the characteristics of emerging markets

(Khanna & Palepu, 2010). By developing a three-market model, it can describe the major differences that distinguish an emerging market from developed and other emerging markets. Emerging markets are characterized by the incompleteness of their market mechanisms, while developed markets have well-structured ones. Hence, by checking the incompleteness of an emerging market, we can capture the differences with developed markets. In fact, many studies have used this theoretical framework to analyze the features of emerging markets (Gao *et al.*, 2017; Hoskisson *et al.*, 2000).

The theoretical framework of institutional voids assumes that companies face three different types of markets: product, labor and financial. First, with respect to the product market, serious institutional voids can be seen in the logistics and distribution channel, which has been a widespread problem in emerging markets (Anderson & Markides, 2007). In emerging markets, there are often no big distributors or transporters that possess a logistics network that covers the country, and such an immature distribution system makes it difficult for companies to transact correctly and fairly with consumers in rural areas. In addition to the distribution channel, the information channel must be considered in emerging markets (Khanna & Palepu, 2010). When a country lacks neutral mass media channels and social media websites are banned or inaccessible, people may not get correct information about the product and, thus, may not engage in an optimal consumption behavior. Moreover, for multinational corporations, it is difficult to communicate with consumers effectively because of the shortage of such media. The possibility of customer contractual default is also a serious problem in emerging markets (Miller *et al.*, 2009) because the customers often have poor solvency as compared to those in developed countries. Furthermore, the shortcomings of the legal system increase the risk of opportunistic behavior. Therefore, a company that enters an emerging market must be prepared to reduce the risk of contractual default.

Second, in the labor market, the two problems that prevent efficient market mechanisms are the lack of skills and incentives. Regarding the quality of labor, the educational infrastructure from primary to higher education is sometimes very poor in emerging countries. Thus, the labor skills are insufficient with respect to highly technological operations, strategic planning, financial trade and structured marketing and sales (London & Hart, 2004; Luo & Tung, 2007), and sometimes, it becomes impossible to conduct business operations in the same manner as in

Table 2.   Types of institutional voids

Market	Institutional void
Product market	Product channel (logistics)
	Information channel (media)
	Contractual default risk
Labor market	Labor skills
	Work motivation
Capital market	Underdeveloped financial market

developed countries (Hoskisson *et al.*, 2000). Furthermore, a company entering an emerging market often faces the problem of local employees' low motivation to work, as they sometimes disregard work because of the lack of social norms or practices to engage in a more modern work style. In addition, they often leave their jobs illegally. In such situations, companies require additional incentive systems to motivate and guide their employees to do their jobs properly (Reficco & Márquez, 2012).

Third, regarding the capital markets, companies often face difficulties in getting funds when the local financial institutions and stock markets are not well developed (Chakrabarty, 2009; Dhanaraj & Khanna, 2011). It requires strenuous efforts to make large investments to construct a new facility, run a big promotion campaign or develop a proprietary distribution network. In such cases, companies must rely on money transfers from their corporate headquarters. However, such money transfers are sometimes banned or restricted. Many emerging nations restrict capital movements for currency and real economic stability (Nugent, 2019). Therefore, it is necessary to keep an eye on the capital flows of multinational companies in developed countries, albeit without malicious intent.

Table 2 summarizes the institutional voids. This framework of institutional voids has been highly regarded as being able to capture the characteristics of emerging markets (Mair *et al.*, 2012; Puffer *et al.*, 2010). In the following section, we will examine how the Yakult Lady method overcomes these problems.

Methodology

We adopt a case study method that derives answers inductively from actual observations. Considering the open-ended nature of the question regarding why the Yakult Lady method works effectively in emerging countries, it seems difficult to generate *a priori* hypotheses from the theory. Thus, we should take an explorative approach to find an answer for the "why-type" question (Miles & Huberman, 1994). In addition, it seems suitable to adopt a qualitative approach because we try to capture the whole structure of the Yakult Lady method and the emerging markets where various factors interact (Yin, 2017). Based on the replication logic of the multiple case study methodology (Eisenhardt, 1989), we observe some of Yakult's overseas business cases and try to identify convergence of the causal mechanisms of the phenomena (Bell *et al.*, 2018). The lack of knowledge about how variables are causally related warrants explorative research based on a small number of samples (Johnson & Foss, 2011). In a replication procedure, first, we listed similar cases within Yakult with respect to emerging markets subsidiaries that sold the product only in that country and maintained good financial performance. Next, those subsidiaries were asked randomly to participate in our survey. The field study started in Indonesia in 2017 and then proceeded to Mexico, China and Brazil during 2017–2018. After completing the Brazil survey, the findings showed convergence of the mechanisms. Thus, our study is based on four cases that have the same properties.

In addition, we also interviewed executives from Yakult's Japanese headquarters to validate our understanding of the mechanism and functions of the Yakult Lady method. Further, we observed the current situation and strategy of Yakult's global business and gained an understanding of how the Yakult Lady method is viewed by its overseas business affiliates. The overview of the field survey is shown in Table 3. In each case, more than two layers of the overseas subsidiary were interviewed: senior managers, middle managers and/or sales agents. In addition, field observations of the agents selling the beverage to consumers were conducted at the same time.

Findings

From our survey of the Yakult subsidiaries in four emerging markets, we have found that the Yakult Lady method possesses various features that respond to institutional voids. Regardless of the conditions of institutional (in)completeness, the Yakult Lady method works effectively because it fills the voids by developing distribution networks, communication channels with customers and labor skills without making huge investments.

Table 3.   Summary of the survey

Case	Data collection method	Date
P.T. YAKULT INDONESIA PERSADA (Indonesia)	Interview	President, Nov. 5, 2015; Oct. 25, 2016
		Board of directors, Nov. 5, 2015; Oct. 25–28, 2016
	Observation	Sales meeting, Nov. 5, 2015; Oct. 25, 2016
		Sales activity, Oct. 26, 2016; Oct. 28, 2016
YAKULT S.A. DE C.V. (Mexico)	Interview	President, Dec. 19, 2017
		Sales director, Dec. 19, 2017
		Agent, Dec. 20, 2017
	Observation	Sales meeting, Dec. 20, 2017
		Sales activity, Dec. 20, 2017
GUANGZHOU YAKULT CO., LTD. (China)	Interview	President, Jan. 11, 2018
		Vice president, Jan. 11, 2018
		Agent, Jan. 12, 2018
	Observation	Sales meeting, Jan. 12, 2018
		Sales activity, Jan. 12, 2018
YAKULT S/A. IND.E COM. (Brazil)	Interview	President, Apr. 19, 2018
		Sales managers, Apr. 19, 2018
		Agent, Apr. 18, 2018
	Observation	Sales meeting, Apr. 18–19, 2018
		Sales activity, Apr. 18–19, 2018
YAKULT HONSHA CO., LTD. (Japan)	Interview	Sales manager, Jan. 22, 2018
		Board of directors, Jan. 22, 2018
	Observation	Sales meeting, Jan. 22, 2018
		Sales activity, Jan. 22, 2018

The summary of the findings is shown in Table 4, with the following sections explaining how the Yakult Lady method tackles each void.

Product Logistics Problem

Three out of the four countries have difficulties with respect to product logistics. In Indonesia, automobiles are unable to enter narrow streets in urban areas, making it difficult to access small shops. In Mexico and Brazil, transportation networks that connect the whole country are not in place, making it difficult to send goods to rural areas. The Yakult Lady

Table 4. Summary of the findings of the study

	Product market voids		
	Product channel (How did the Yakult Lady method respond?)	**Information channel (How did the Yakult Lady method respond?)**	**Contractual default of customers (How did the Yakult Lady method respond?)**
Indonesia	Narrow alleys that cars cannot enter (Ladies enter on foot)	There are too many mass media commercials compared to the market size (Ladies give detailed information about the product to the customers face-to-face while having an enjoyable chat)	Consumers and distributors sometimes fall into default when they use credit (Yakult only conducts on-the-spot cash transactions)
Mexico	Transporation companies do not cover all rural areas (Yakult built its own network by hiring agents in rural areas)	There are too many mass media commercials compared to the market size (Ladies give detailed information about the product to customers face-to-face while having an enjoyable chat)	Consumers and distributors sometimes fall into default when they use credit (Yakult only conducts on-the-spot cash transactions)
Brazil	Transporation companies do not cover all rural areas (Yakult built its own network by hiring agents in rural areas)	There are too many mass media commercials compared to the market size (Ladies give detailed information about the product to customers face-to-face while having an enjoyable chat)	Consumers and distributors seldom fall into default (Even though there is no risk of default, Yakult only conducts on-the-spot cash transactions in most case)
China	No difficulty (While local transportation is available, Yakult still applies the same method)	No difficulty (While there is no difficulty in using mass media, Yakult makes the agents play a role in explaining the product)	Consumers and distributors seldom fall into default (Yakult conducts on-the-spot cash transaction)

(Continued)

Table 4.   (Continued)

	Labor market voids		Capital markets
	Human skills	Incentives	Difficulty in corporate finance
Indonesia	Low marketing/sales skills (Comprehensive and continuous training programs and complementary use of social capital)	Low motivation of workers, sometimes susceptible to high risk (Use of individual sales agent contracts and strategies to rebalance risk and return)	Local financial market is weak and volatile (Yakult does not rely on the local financial market and uses its own cash savings)
Mexico	Low marketing/sales skills (Comprehensive and continuous training programs and complementary use of social capital)	Low motivation of workers (Use of individual sales agent contracts)	Local financial market is weak and volatile (Yakult does not rely on the local financial market and uses its own cash savings)
Brazil	Low marketing/sales skills (Comprehensive and continuous training programs and complementary use of social capital)	Low motivation of workers (Use of individual sales agent contracts)	Local financial market is weak and volatile (Yakult does not rely on the local financial market and uses its own cash savings)
China	Low marketing/sales skills (Comprehensive and continuous training programs and complementary use of social capital)	Low motivation of workers (Use of individual sales agent contracts)	Local financial market is moderately structured (Even when the local financial system is adequate, Yakult does not rely on it and uses its own cash savings)

method overcomes such difficulties and provides access to consumers living in harder to reach areas. In all four countries, including China (that had no transportation problems), Yakult established its own distribution network without using the local distribution system. In addition, all four of Yakult's local subsidiaries divide their respective countries into very small sales areas. One local woman is hired from each area to be the "Yakult Lady" in charge of the sales for the area, where she sells the products on foot or by bicycle. In addition, Yakult set up hundreds of distribution bases throughout the four countries in order to distribute the product to the women. As a result of this in-house distribution network, Yakult is able to deliver products to consumers regardless of the institutional voids in the local logistics system. In Indonesia, the Yakult Ladies can enter narrow alleys in the capital city of Jakarta, where products cannot be delivered by car. In Mexico and Brazil, while transportation companies do not cover rural areas with low population density, Yakult can reach these areas using the Yakult Ladies without relying on the local transportation companies. Even in China, while there are only a few difficulties in beverage logistics, Yakult still takes advantage of the Yakult Lady method. Considering the operations in the four countries, we can conclude that the Yakult Lady method enables the company to reach consumers in each country regardless of the development level of the distribution channel.

Information Channel Problem

Regarding the response to the information channel problem, the Yakult Lady Method functions as a medium that can directly communicate information to individuals. Although most of beverages sold by Yakult are healthy functional beverages (Corbo *et al.*, 2014), consumers are often unaware of these functions. To overcome this situation, Yakult has given the role of explaining the function of its beverages to its sales agents. Every day, the women receive training on the product information for their sales base and how to convey it to the consumers. In each of the four countries we observed, the agent communicates the product information directly to customers when selling the beverage. This method not only compensates for the shortage of media but also conveys more information than that provided by radio or television. In three of the countries (excluding China), the use of mass media entailed too high of a cost compared to the size of the market. Thus, Yakult utilized direct communication between the agents and the customers to provide information about the function of its beverages. In China, in contrast, the balance between the fees incurred and the influence of the commercial mass media was reasonable. However, Yakult still relies on extensive instruction from the Yakult Ladies in China as it believes that direct communication between the agent and the customer is crucial in helping consumers understand and appreciate the products' merits.

Contractual Default Risk

Yakult adopts on-the-spot cash transactions in every market to avoid the problem of contractual default with low-income customers. In three of the countries (excluding Brazil), Yakult does not conduct transactions via credit or monthly contracts. Instead, it has a rule of transacting cash sales on the spot, adopting the same rule in its transactions with the agents. Only when the agent reports and deposits the previous day's sales revenue is her stock replenished with the products to sell for the day. Therefore, Yakult can smoothly receive the sales revenue within a day in cash, with its local subsidiaries never facing the problem of default or suffering from cash shortage. However, Yakult accepts credit transactions in Brazil. Since credit transactions are predominant there, Yakult has had to adapt to this situation. Its subsidiary's expatriate manager from Japan responded to this special situation after observing and analyzing the business structure of the local people. He developed a method specific to Brazil, where the agent and the customer deepened their personal relationship through daily communication, with the agent simultaneously investigating the creditworthiness of the customer and building a long-term relationship of trust to facilitate smooth transactions.

Human Work Skills

The local human relationships of Yakult Ladies also play an important role by complementing their marketing and sales skills. In all four countries, Yakult does not require a potential agent to have the latter skills. Instead, it assesses their human and local relationships. If a potential agent has strong personal relationships, she is likely to develop further friendship networks with customers in her sales area. Before selling, the Yakult Lady and her manager decide the sales area that she is responsible for and develop the route within that area. She spends her workdays (usually from

Monday to Saturday) walking through it, continuously meeting her customers on the route in front of their houses every week. Even if the customer does not buy anything, she spends a considerable amount of time
talking about the product and the health of the customer's family while
having an enjoyable chat. Thus, the friendship with that customer is developed gradually. Her original personal relationships, in addition to those
newly developed, contribute to improving her sales revenues. Further, as
an important part of the Yakult Lady method, Yakult introduced comprehensive training programs for its ladies. Based on the premise that the
women hired in all countries have a low level of business skills, Yakult
intensively trains them on sales talk, calculations, accounting, marketing
planning and troubleshooting. Even in countries where the women do not
require special training to start a business, they have to undergo training.
Yakult is keen on establishing a long-lasting relationship with each agent;
thus, it emphasizes spending a considerable amount of time investing in
human capital.

Work Motivation

As pointed out in the previous studies, a distinguishing feature of the
Yakult Lady method is the sharing of business risk with the agents through
the sales agent contract. In other words, the Yakult Lady is not a regular
employee of Yakult but an independent individual business entity that is
an equal partner of Yakult. We have confirmed that this method has been
adopted in all four cases. The Japanese expatriate managers of the subsidiaries in the four countries recognized that the contract is the central feature of the Yakult Lady method. They reported that Yakult ladies work
using their own efforts, and thus, they succeed in business and life by their
own efforts. Yakult's headquarters clearly regard it as a mechanism that
provides the agents with the incentive to put in the effort needed to
improve sales. Interestingly, our observations have clarified that Yakult's
local subsidiaries often adopt additional mechanisms to balance incentive
and risk. If the company were to impose a complete incentive-based payment structure on the women, they would suffer from low earnings even
when working hard. In other words, the risk of receiving lower earnings
becomes too high when the incentive structure is strong. In Indonesia,
there was previously a large gap between the high-performing agents and
the poor-performing ones. Since poor performers often left the company,
Yakult suffered from a high turnover rate. After experiencing this issue in

some countries, Yakult developed another incentive scheme to comple-ment the basic approach of giving incentives using agent contracts. For example, if the agent cannot generate sufficient earnings, Yakult's regular employees try to improve it by (1) adjusting her sales area and (2) sup-porting the sales activities. Regarding the sales area, the local Yakult subsidiary has complete control over it, as the agents are not allowed to change it without permission. Instead, if some agents claim that they can-not make enough sales, Yakult adjusts each agent's sales area slightly so that all can earn enough income. In addition, when an agent cannot achieve enough sales, the sales support staff intensively helps her improve sales by giving advice and sometimes even selling directly with her.

Underdeveloped Financial Market

Regarding the financial aspect of the Yakult Lady method, this study has found that Yakult has never made a large investment in any country. The company always started with a very small operation using about ten agents, covering small areas of the country, maintaining a positive cash flow and always using the earnings for investment (internal cash reserve). Thus, Yakult's operation in each country increased gradually. For exam-ple, the Indonesia subsidiary, which was established in 1991, started with a dozen ladies initially. Subsequently, about 50 additional ladies were hired, increasing to 500 ladies in the year 2000, 1,000 in 2007 and 5,000 in 2013. It should be noted that the Yakult Lady method itself is a mecha-nism that never cause deficits, unless the company spends too much money on investment. Yakult's cost structure mainly consists of the pay-ment for the agents. However, Yakult Ladies earn their incomes by selling the beverages themselves. Thus, the labor cost never surpasses the reve-nue of the products.

Expatriate Learning for Local Adaptation

Finally, although it differs from direct measurement against institutional voids, the fact that Japanese expatriate managers have the authority to change the method to adapt to the local situation seems to be the key to success in all of the observed cases. Yakult developed a standard form of the Yakult Lady method for overseas in the 1980s. When the company enters an overseas market, it introduces this standardized approach for each country. However, expatriate managers have been tasked with adjusting the Yakult Lady method according to the local circumstances. Thus, by combining the in-depth understanding of the Yakult Lady method from Japan with an understanding of the local situation, expats are able to competently modify the method.

Discussion

Why Does the Yakult Lady Method Work in Various Emerging Markets?

According to the findings of the field-based investigation, the Yakult Lady method has performed very well in all the observed countries. It indicates that the Yakult lady method can work, regardless of the readiness of the institutions. As summarized in Table 4, the institutional environment that Yakult faced in each country was very different, nevertheless the method has succeeded in obtaining market share in every country. Drawing on this fact, it can be said that the Yakult Lady method is less affected by the institutional settings. Why does the Yakult Lady method avert the effect of institutional differences? From the observations, it is because the Yakult method fills the institutional gaps with its own resources: the Yakult Ladies themselves. By organizing and training local women, Yakult develops a system that works as a distribution network, information channel, rich pool of skilled labor and money collection. These functions of the Yakult Lady make up for the vulnerability of institutional settings in the product, labor and capital markets. Therefore, the answer to the question of why the Yakult Lady is effective in emerging market countries is that it has created a system that acts as a substitute for local market institutions. Interestingly, as we have reviewed in its history, it is no coincidence that Yakult adopted such a business style. However, it can be said that the Yakult Lady performs well in today's emerging markets because it was developed when Japan's institutional environment was less mature.

Theoretical Implications for Institutional Voids Research

In addition to being a success story, the Yakult case brings important theoretical implications for the study about institutional voids. That is, it gives a hint of how to overcome (or take advantage of) institutional voids. Past studies mainly have investigated the institutional voids themselves: how they are, what they come from and how they affect corporate behavior (Castellacci, 2015; Leff, 1978; Puffer & McCarthy, 2011). Regarding the business strategy for those voids, existing studies have concluded that companies should respond by changing some strategic variables (e.g. product design, marketing mix, recruiting policy, and finance policy) according to the state of voids (Khanna & Palepu, 2010; Mair *et al.*, 2012; Puffer *et al.*, 2010). However, such an approach requires companies to redesign different business strategies each time, in each emerging market. Yakult's case, on the contrary, suggests that if a company wants to be successful in many emerging market countries, it should prepare a business model that works regardless of the state of the voids. Here, it must be emphasized that the Yakult Lady method is not the only answer, but there might be the other business models that meet the above conditions. Unlike previous studies, our review of the Yakult case suggests that a business model that does not depend on the state of institutional voids may have a competitive advantage in emerging markets.

In addition, this study of Yakult also suggests that veteran expatriate managers who understand the company's way of business and the local market play a key role in business success in emerging markets. In the case of Yakult, the expatriate managers are fully educated in Japan regarding the operations of the Yakult Lady method for at least a few years, then they are sent to an emerging market country to conduct business and learn about the local situation there for more than three years. Afterward, he/she adjusts the Yakult Lady method to be in line with the local situation. Using this active refinement approach to the Yakult Lady Method, Yakult has been able to fully adapt to each market. Such a role for expatriate managers has also been suggested in other studies (Briscoe *et al.*, 2012).

Limitations and Implications

We need to further analyze the advantages and disadvantages of the Yakult Lady method as compared to other business systems in emerging markets. We should also consider the possibility of duplicating the Yakult Lady method at other companies and improve on its limitations. Although some follow-up examples, including Hindustan Unilever, have already appeared (Rangan & Rajan, 2007), there is room to consider whether it is widely applicable. Thus, further qualitative investigations that broaden the scope of observation are needed. Moreover, if a certain number of replication cases appear in the future, it will be necessary to verify them through quantitative analysis. Finally, we would like to mention the practical implications of this study. This study suggests that it is necessary to establish a comprehensive method that works regardless of the condition of institutional voids to generate profit from several emerging markets. In the case of Yakult, it has constructed its distribution networks regardless of the situation of the existing ones and sold its products by utilizing the local communities regardless of the skill level of the workers. Adaptation to local conditions by expatriate managers has also contributed greatly to its success. However, this method has been applicable in various countries because it has characteristics that are not overly influenced by the conditions of each country. Such a mechanism may be created for sales, production, logistics or research and development. To overcome the institutional voids, we should aim at constructing a business system that does not depend on the status of institutional development.

References

Anderson, J. & Markides, C. (2007). Strategic innovation at the base of the pyramid. *MIT Sloan Management Review*, 49(1), 83–88.

Bell, E., Bryman, A. & Harley, B. (2018). *Business Research Methods*. Oxford University Press, Oxford.

Briscoe, D., Tarique, I. & Schuler, R. (2012). *International Human Resource Management: Policies and Practices for Multinational Enterprises*. Routledge, London.

Cahn, P.S. (2006). Building down and dreaming up. *American Ethnologist*, 33(1), 126–142.

Castellacci, F. (2015). Institutional voids or organizational resilience? Business groups, innovation, and market development in Latin America. *World Development*, 70, 43–58.

Chakrabarty, S. (2009). The influence of national culture and institutional voids on family ownership of large firms: A country level empirical study. *Journal of International Management*, 15(1), 32–45.

Corbo, M.R., Bevilacqua, A., Petruzzi, L., Casanova, F.P. & Sinigaglia, M. (2014). Functional beverages: the emerging side of functional foods: commercial trends, research, and health implications. *Comprehensive Reviews in Food Science and Food Safety*, 13(6), 1192–1206.

Dhanaraj, C. & Khanna, T. (2011). Transforming mental models on emerging markets. *Academy of Management Learning & Education*, 10(4), 684–701.

Eisenhardt, K.M. (1989). Building theories from case study research. *Academy of Management Review*, 14(4), 532–550.

Gao, C., Zuzul, T., Jones, G. & Khanna, T. (2017). Overcoming institutional voids: A reputation-based view of long-run survival. *Strategic Management Journal*, 38(11), 2147–2167.

Ghalib, A., Hossain, F. & Arun, T. (2009). Social responsibility, business strategy and development: the case of Grameen-Danone Foods Limited. *Australasian Accounting, Business and Finance Journal*, 3(4), 1.

Goyaland, A. & Gupta, A. (2015) Customer barriers and product disposition in probiotic market — A case study of Yakult in India. From the desk of the chief editor, 20.

Horn, S.A. (2009). Product adoption and innovation diffusion: the case of Japanese marketing to China. *Asia Pacific Business Review*, 15(3), 389–409.

Hoskisson, R.E., Eden, L., Lau, C.M. & Wright, M. (2000). Strategy in emerging economies. *Academy of Management Journal*, 43(3), 249–267.

Jacob, S. & Kwok, P. (2011). Improving lives in the base of pyramid, profitably. *Social Space*, 48–53.

Johansson, J.K. & Nonaka, I. (1996). *Relentless: The Japanese Way of Marketing.* Harper Business, New York City.

Jonsson, A. & Foss, N.J. (2011). International expansion through flexible replication: Learning from the internationalization experience of IKEA. *Journal of International Business Studies*, 42(9), 1079–1102.

Khanna, T. & Palepu, K.G. (2010). *Winning in Emerging Markets: A Road Map for Strategy and Execution.* Harvard Business Press, Massachusetts.

Leff, N.H. (1978). Industrial organization and entrepreneurship in the developing countries: The economic groups. *Economic Development and Cultural Change*, 26(4), 661–675.

Leliveld, A. & Knorringa, P. (2018). Frugal innovation and development research. *The European Journal of Development Research*, 30(1), 1–16.

London, T. & Hart, S.L. (2004). Reinventing strategies for emerging markets: beyond the transnational model. *Journal of International Business Studies*, 35(5), 350–370.

Luo, Y. & Tung, R.L. (2007). International expansion of emerging market enterprises: A springboard perspective. *Journal of International Business Studies*, 38(4), 481–498.

Mair, J., Martí, I. & Ventresca, M.J. (2012). Building inclusive markets in rural Bangladesh: How intermediaries work institutional voids. *Academy of Management Journal*, 55(4), 819–850.

Mathur, M.K., Swami, S. & Bhatnagar, S. (2016). BOP business models and strategy. *Amity Journal of Management Research*, 1(1), 110–123.

Miles, M.B., Huberman, A.M., Huberman, M.A. & Huberman, M. (1994). *Qualitative Data Analysis: An Expanded Sourcebook.* Sage, California.

Miller, D., Lee, J., Chang, S. & Le Breton-Miller, I. (2009). Filling the institutional void: The social behavior and performance of family vs non-family technology firms in emerging markets. *Journal of International Business Studies*, 40(5), 802–817.

Mizuo, J. (2016). Global CSR centered on BOP business and CSV: A consideration of its types and development. *Surugadaikeizaironsyu*, 25(2), 43–87.

Nakagawa, K. & Imagawa, T. (2019). Women who fill the institutional voids: Why does Yakult succeed in obtaining emerging markets? In Camacho, L. and Singh, S. (eds.), *Proceedings of the Academy of Business and Emerging Markets (ABEM) 2019 Conference.* Canada, pp. 52–60. https://www.abem.ca/wp-content/uploads/2019/07/abem-2019-proceedings.pdf [Accessed in March 2020].

Nugent, R.J. (2019). Restrictions on short-term capital inflows and the response of direct investment. *Eastern Economic Journal*, 45(3), 350–383.

Prahalad, C.K. (2006). *The Fortune at the Bottom of the Pyramid.* Pearson Education India, Tamil Nadu.

Pratt, M.G. (2000). The good, the bad, and the ambivalent: Managing identification among Amway distributors. *Administrative Science Quarterly*, 45(3), 456–493.

Puffer, S.M., McCarthy, D.J. & Boisot, M. (2010). Entrepreneurship in Russia and China: The impact of formal institutional voids. *Entrepreneurship Theory and Practice*, 34(3), 441–467.

Puffer, S.M. & McCarthy, D.J. (2011). Two decades of Russian business and management research: An institutional theory perspective. *Academy of Management Perspectives*, 25(2), 21–36.

Raja, B.R. & Arunachalam, K.D. (2011). Market potential for probiotic nutritional supplements in India. *African Journal of Business Management*, 5(14), 5418–5423.

Rangan, V.K. & Rajan, R. (2007). *Unilever in India: Hindustan Lever's Project Shakti-Marketing FMCG to the Rural Consumer.* Boston, MA: Harvard Business School.

Reficco, E. & Márquez, P. (2012). Inclusive networks for building BOP markets. *Business & Society*, 51(3), 512–556.

Sugawara, H. (2010). Japanese business and poverty reduction *Society and Business Review*, 5(2), 198–216.

Yakult Honsha Website (n.d.). Retrieved from; https://www.yakult.co.jp/english [Accessed on February 2, 2020].

Yin, R.K. (2017). *Case Study Research and Applications: Design and Methods.* Sage Publications, California.

https://doi.org/10.1142/9789811221750_0004

Chapter 4

Artificial Intelligence and Cyber Security: A New Pathway for Growth in Emerging Economies via the Knowledge Economy?

Meera Sarma[*,‡], Thomas Matheus[†] and Chaminda Senaratne[†]

*University of Liverpool, Liverpool L69 3BX, UK

†Northumbria University, Newcastle-upon-Tyne, NE1 8ST, UK

‡meera.sarma@liverpool.ac.uk

For emerging economies, artificial intelligence (AI) and cyber security play a vital role as a catalyst to accelerate growth while providing mechanisms to protect and support critical infrastructure. In this chapter, we examine a critical question of what the implications are of the use and growth of AI and cyber security in the context of emerging economies. The chapter finds that that the application of AI tools and techniques to specific cyber security issues, such as intelligent malware and the rapid evolution of cyber-attacks, offers solutions to complex challenges faced by emerging economies. It could potentially underpin solutions for the protection of critical sectors such as education and health (cyber security) when offering a new pathway to innovation and entrepreneurship (AI), enabling co-operation and communication in the new knowledge economy. We make the first attempt to conceptualize the AI–cyber security relationship in the context of economic growth. We distil and connect the specific elements of AI and cyber security that offer an advantage to emerging countries through improved output and increased income through a conceptual framework and explain the impact it would have on specific economic factors and economic performance.

Introduction

This chapter offers an analysis of aspects relating to artificial intelligence (AI) and cyber security and their impact on emerging economies. It examines a key question of the implications of the development of AI and cyber security in the context of emerging economies. In the first section, we discuss how AI influences emerging economies and what the future holds for emerging economies based on AI developments. In the second section, we discuss a number of cyber security aspects in emerging economies and some of the future developments in cyber security in emerging economies. In the third section, we relate the recent developments in AI and cyber security in the context of emerging economies. Subsequently, we offer conclusion and directions for future research, facilitating the development of a knowledge economy (using AI and cyber security). Knowledge economy refers to an emerging economic structure, in which success is increasingly based upon the effective utilization of intangible assets such as knowledge, skills and innovative potential as the key resource for competitive advantage.

Literature Review

Knowledge Economy and Emerging Economies

The main element of a knowledge economy is a greater dependence on intellectual capabilities as opposed to natural resources or physical inputs. This needs to be coalesced with efforts to incorporate advances in various stages of the manufacturing process, including R&D management, the manufacturing facility and customer interfaces (Powell & Snellman, 2004). An emerging economy is an economy that grows rapidly with structurally changing industries, promising but volatile markets and a regulatory framework that undergoes drastic and sometimes, unexpected, transformations (Hoskisson *et al.*, 2000; Liu *et al.*, 2011). Given the need for global competitiveness and the ever more accelerating digitalization across industrial sectors (Dalenogare *et al.*, 2018), AI and cyber security might be appropriate focal areas for existing knowledge economies in emerging markets and for transitioning toward knowledge-intensive modes of production of emerging markets. The knowledge economy relates to a wide range of activities (Powell & Snellman, 2004); for example, the rise of new science-based industries and their role in social and economic change (Machlup, 1962); the kinds of industries that can be classed as being knowledge intensive and the contribution to economic growth of these industries (Gordon, 2000); and intra-organizational knowledge management (Nonaka & Takeuchi, 1995). The intention of this chapter is to offer a contribution to the first strand of theories from an emerging economy perspective.

Innovation and Emerging Economies

Various researchers call for developing innovation research across economic sectors and geographic regions (Crossan & Apaydin, 2010; Hall & Rosenberg, 2010). For instance, firms in emerging economies find it challenging to survive without knowing how to provide services to global customers (Dimitratos *et al.*, 2014). Although emerging economies have a necessity to develop innovations (Levitt, 1983), their innovation dynamics are complex and differ based on the industry and the territory (Asheim & Gertler, 2006). Furthermore, emerging economies face limitations, e.g. political and economic uncertainty, in relation to their ability to innovate (Castellacci, 2015; Webb *et al.*, 2013). In this chapter, we treat AI and cyber security as innovations, which appear to be relevant for emerging economies. We highlight how both types of innovation related to the context of emerging economies and subsequently, tie this in with the knowledge economy in emerging markets.

AI and Emerging Economies

AI is a volume of computer science. It focuses on the development of intellectual technologies that operate and react like humans. AI is also a division of computer science and its purpose is to create intellectual machines (Chowdhry, 2018). The field of AI recently gained more momentum because new AI methods such as machine learning, modern deep learning and natural processing of formless data-advanced technology and algorithms. As such, it has transformed a vital part of the technology industry. Further, AI is very mechanical and specialized and it has been applied in various fields, e.g. medicinal diagnosis, the stock market, robotics, legal processes as well as research and development. On the one hand, Rasheed (2018) identified a continuous automation of occupations over the following years. Various jobs appear to be at risk. Some of these jobs are of an administrative, a clerical or a manufacturing nature. Others are in telemarketing and data entry. On the other hand, societies have managed to integrate some of the changes introduced by AI, which led to new job creation. In short, it appears that high-volume and repetitive jobs are at risk of being replaced by AI, whereas AI might not readily replace jobs involving leadership, creativity and problem solving (Nabi, 2019). A number of concerns exist regarding the fast growth of AI and the diffusion of automation across the planet (including in emerging economies). Below, we will provide an understanding of the influence of AI on the workforce in emerging economies. We also offer a view on what the growth of AI means for the workforce in emerging economies.

AI appears to be an obvious threat to emerging economies, such as China, Thailand and Malaysia, who rely heavily on exports. AI seems to impose a higher threat on economies that are even less developed, such as Cambodia and Myanmar, as well as on economies that have been building labor-intensive industrial areas of a substantial scale, such as India and Bangladesh. The issue for emerging economies is that AI threatens known and established growth strategies (Nabi, 2019).

Crabtree (2018) suggests that across 32 industrial economies, 14% of jobs can be transformed into automated jobs. This is suggested in relation to mechanical robots and AI software performing interpretations and data analysis. Although automation is in its infancy in many emerging economies, there appears to be an accelerated adoption of AI and robotics across Asian countries. In comparison to the USA and South Korea, China's ratios of industrial robots per employee are one-third and one-10th, respectively. It appears though that a raft of AI technologies has already been encroaching on low- and middle-income economies as well (Crabtree, 2018), for example, the use of liquid crystal displays (LCDs) at the Taiwanese iPhone producer Foxconn to automate one in five jobs or the AI innovation referred to as shoeboots, in the textile and garment producing industry.

Green (2017) suggests that robots and automation are likely to replace low-skilled labor and intensive industrialization in a middle-income country, such as Bangladesh. In the future, this is likely to affect five million workers in the garment industry. Higher cognitive and technical skills may also be required for jobs earning higher wages. However, such skills are not readily available in middle-income economies. On top of this, various emerging economies — for example, Pakistan, Egypt, Malaysia and Thailand — are struggling to cope with unemployed and underemployed workforces. Putting this together implies that emerging economies, impacted by such developments, will have to increase their AI skill sets besides being at a less developed industrialization stage.

Organizations may begin to implement AI at their current locations, leaving economies operating with large numbers of unskilled workers in a precarious situation. Subsequently, large groups of young unskilled workers may turn from being an asset into a liability, should AI developments permeate various industries of emerging economies (Nabi, 2019). AI will also impact the service industry. Leung (2018) opines that in service-dominant professions and industries in the USA — for example, call centers — 6% of all jobs will be automated via AI. Such a degree of automation is likely to have a severe impact on emerging economies, for instance the Philippines, in which this sector employs 1.2 million workers, who earn 8% of the national income. In the past, in contrast to this, regions like Asia and Latin America have been able to benefit positively from various technological advancements in the health, housing and food industries. As a consequence of this, emerging economies have to develop the prerequisite engineering knowledge in AI in order to avoid being unable to benefit from the application of AI developments in the future (Leung, 2018).

The exact degree to which AI and automation will impact emerging economies is uncertain; however, it might be worthwhile for such economies to harness new technological innovations to avoid an ever-increasing skills gap. It appears that it is insufficient to solely rely in developing export-oriented industrialization processes and that it will be vital to adopt a multifaceted strategy, which incorporates relevant developments in AI and automation in emerging economies (Yusuf, 2017). As economies move toward rapid digitalization, including AI applications, cyber security is another area of concern.

Cyber Security and Emerging Economies

Cyber security has been an area of interest among both academics and practitioners due to the growing threat of cyber-attacks. Cyber security is defined as *the organization and collection of resources, processes, and structures used to protect cyberspace and cyberspace-enabled systems from occurrences that misalign de jure from de facto property rights* (Craigen *et al.*, 2014). With the increased use of digital devices and the Internet that affect our personal and professional lives, we are exposed to cyber-attacks more than ever.

The deeply embedded nature of cyberspace into all other industry sectors enabling interconnectedness makes it difficult to separate cyberspace from these sectors and to identify the vulnerabilities. This increasing complexity of the cyberspace has created new economic, social and political possibilities (Clemente, 2013).

While we are benefitted from the growing complexity of cyberspace and also exposed to growing cyber threats, Singer and Friedman (2014) highlight the level of "cyber security knowledge gap" among the top-level government officials citing examples from the US and Australia. They also claim that even though cyber security touches every aspect of private and public sector concern, only the young and the computer savvy are well engaged with it (Singer & Friedman, 2014). This indicates the need for cyber security education. As far as government initiatives to deal with cyber security are concerned, the ITU (2019) survey reported that a total of 53 countries demonstrated a high level of national cyber security commitment. The United Kingdom (Rank 1), the United States of America (Rank 2) and France (Rank 3) were the top three GCI most committed countries globally in 2018. Even though cyber security models of those countries might not be universally applicable, those models (for example, the US model) could be used to identify areas of progress and potential pitfalls for countries that would like to emulate them (Clemente, 2013).

ITU (2019) statistics further indicate that cybercrime legislation is globally well implemented and about 177 countries (91%) have cybercrime legislation. When it comes to non-western countries, in the Africa region 38 out of 44, in the Americas region 32 out of 35, in the Arab States region 18 out of 22, and in the Asia-Pacific region 35 out of 38 countries have cybercrime legislation (ITU, 2019). As far as the computer emergency response teams (CERT) that deal with cyber-attacks are concerned, ITU (2019) reported that, in 2018, the African region has the lowest number of countries (13 out of 44 countries that responded), nearly 50% of the countries in the Americas region (17 out of 35) and the Arab States region (10 out of 22) have a national CERT. It also shows that the Asia-Pacific region (24 out of 38) and the Commonwealth of Independent States (CIS) region have more countries with a national CERT.

However, ITU (2019) points out that just adopting laws would be insufficient and governments need to use laws as a framework to implement strategies to enhance cyber security. Growing digitalization and cyber security concerns might have important implications for emerging economies. For example, Asia is leading the development of the digital economy in emerging markets adopting such technologies as blockchain, cloud computing and e-commerce (OECD, 2019). While the private sector is playing a key role in these areas, further government policy actions related to digital trade, investment in digital technologies education and developing digital infrastructure are needed, and such policy action would also include addressing cyber security concerns (OECD, 2019). This is particularly important, as national cyber security strategy seems to play a key role when it comes to motivating cyber security investment in organizations.

Baker (2014) claims that emerging economies like Brazil, Russia, India and China suffer economically more than economically developed nations from cybercrime. Cybercrimes have not only financial but also non-financial implications for emerging economies. The former comprises financial losses due to cyber-attacks and the latter includes, for example, loss of customer confidence, negative publicity and loss of confidential data (Antonescu & Birău, 2015). Therefore, developing cyber security in emerging economies would boost their economic development (Baker, 2014). Extending Harknett and Stever (2009), US-based cyber security triad, i.e. intergovernmental relations, private sector partners, and cyber security citizenship, Baker (2014) proposed a model that would be more applicable to developing cyber security in emerging economies. The model includes four factors: foreign government relations, internal governance, private sector partners and active cyber citizenship (Baker, 2014). We have already touched upon internal governance under government regulations and private sector partners under public–private partnership in developing cyber security. Developing active cyber citizenship needs investment in developing a country's citizen's technical talent that would contribute to national cyber security as well as to the economic development of a country (Baker, 2014). Thus, developing cyber citizenship would help reduce the cyber security knowledge gap mentioned above. Foreign government relations, the next dimension of Baker's (2014) model, is particularly important for emerging economies given possible resource constraints in developing cyber security (Tagert, 2010). In addition, collaborations with foreign governments reduce possible cyber wars between emerging economies and developed economies and also such conflicts among emerging economies. The complex nature of cyberspace that does not limit to one geographic region also demands such collaboration in promoting cyber security.

With the ongoing digital revolution, Brazil, one of the BRICS countries (Brazil, Russia, India, China and South-Africa), witnesses a rapid increase in Internet access and mobile phone subscriptions with more than half the population of 200 million people currently online (Diniz *et al.*, 2014). In turn, the number of computer incidents reported to Brazil's Central Computer Security Incident Response Team has increased where at least 75% of Brazilian Internet users claim to have been victims of some form of cybercrime (Diniz *et al.*, 2014). However, these authors point out that there are knowledge gaps in dealing with cybercrimes (e.g. identifying cybercriminals and responding to cyber-attacks) in Brazil.

Russia, another BRICS country, saw a significant increase in the number of Internet users from 25% in 2007 to 76% in 2018 of the country's population, and this dynamic expansion of the Internet, e-commerce and networked digital systems, the general number of crimes committed using computerized telecommunications technologies increased from 1,300 to about 175,000, which is a 53% increase from 2018 to 2019 (Sukharenko, 2019). The Digital Economy of the Russian Federation program approved in 2017 identifies the growth of cybercrime domestically and internationally, the increased capabilities of external actors and the lack of qualified security experts as the main challenges that impede the development of the digital economy (Sukharenko, 2019). In the case of India, the country has reported a relatively high score in all four dimensions where the country is strong and deeply involved in the international arena economically and militarily, developing cyber infrastructure rapidly due to a relatively stable government structure, having high levels of FDI and possessing a very active cyber population (Baker, 2014).

KPMG (2016) report that in China in the first half of 2016, 37% of Internet users have suffered an economic loss due to various types of Internet fraud and 84% have experienced some sort of negative impact from personal information leakage. Thus, China has established

Cyber Security Laws and assigned the regulatory responsibilities of cyber security to the National Network and Information Office (overall coordination for cyber security supervision and management); and the Telecommunications Department of the State Council, the Ministry of Public Security and other related departments (responsible for cyber security protection and supervision within each department's remit (KPMG, 2016). South Africa, set up The Cyber security Hub in 2012 and it is South Africa's National Computer Security Incident Response Team (CSIRT) that works with stakeholders from the government, the private sector, civil society and the public with a view to identifying and countering cyber security threats (Mooi & Botha, 2016). Overall, major emerging economics like the BRICS nations have identified cyber security as a major element in achieving economic development.

AI and Cyber Security as a Catalyst for Growth in Emerging Markets

For emerging economies, AI and cyber security, hold promise, as a catalyst to accelerate growth and overcome hurdles in key areas of societal development such as infrastructure, healthcare and education. The employment of AI technologies in this field would enable dealing with cyber threats and is essential in safeguarding critical infrastructure. In recent years, advanced malware and rapidly evolving cyber capabilities require "intelligent software" that can adapt, is flexible and has the capacity to learn (Zhang *et al.*, 2019). Although various AI techniques are being used in the assessment of cyber defense systems, there is a need for advanced evolving solutions and assessment of situations, automated knowledge systems and intelligent decision support functions, for issues that are more complicated. Scholars (Muller Jr., 2009) have suggested that there is a need for intelligent networks and systems that can "self-defend" thereby increasing long-term resilience. Experts in the field of cyber security also contend that the simultaneous occurrences of exploits, outages and vulnerabilities, around the world, would require rapid analysis of events and decision-making as it would put enormous amount of stress on systems and in this regard, developing countries are particularly vulnerable (Tyugu, 2011).

A report from the US Department of Defense indicates that subversions of sophisticated hardware and software systems are extraordinarily difficult to detect through testing and inspection. This led the Task Force to conclude that deeper intelligence about adversaries' offensive software and hardware tools is essential to counter high-end, state-sponsored cyber threats, because it can help focus US efforts on likely targets of compromise (Gosler & Von Thaer, 2013). The report suggests that intelligent deep learning is needed to identify and understand the development of cyber adversary tools and further automation to counter possible threats and accurate assessment of cyber adversary plans and threats.

The use of AI tools in conjunction with advanced cyber security plays a significant role in offering solutions to issues such as susceptibility of systems for attacks, absence of a predict–prevent–defend system to foresee potential threats, the need for continuous monitoring and awareness of situations to mitigate attacks, the need for comprehensive, deep-rooted knowledge about threats for decision support and the ability to detect anomalies and unusual behavior of the use of systems and network traffic and the ability to spot insider threats. The inability to recognize and analyze patterns from different sources and streams of data not only the management of dynamic data from hundreds of sources and devices but the need to develop a dynamic map of the depth and breadth of data received into actionable intelligence tells us that these are core challenges faced by most countries and in particular developing economies.

A key challenge for developing economies in particular would be the lack of trained cyber security personnel (Gosler & Von Thaer, 2013). The presence of a skills gap, lack of training in AI and advanced automation and the training and retention of staff in this area need further consideration and analysis, particularly in the light of future demographic trends and the changing threat landscapes.

It is important to note that while applications of AI such as intelligent agents, expert systems, neural networks, robotics are currently being used to learn, seek and offer solutions to cyber-related challenges, there are other areas of technology and science that offer tools and techniques for further consideration. It is possible that in the future AI can be combined with other disciplines to provide disruptive innovations to fields such as cyber security. For example, advances in behavioral sciences brain activity mapping and neuro-imaging could be used to understand human behavior better and offer advanced solutions to the issue of insider threats. It is necessary therefore to explore the development of affiliated fields such as psychology and mathematics relevant in particular for certain developing countries such as India, as noted by scholars (Kalyanakrishnan *et al.*, 2018) that there are about 300 start-ups in India with a focus on AI with over USD 100 million invested in them. This number, however, is low in comparison to countries like the US and China, where investments total over USD 4 and 3 billion, respectively. Lack of datasets and talent are both challenges that start-ups will have to negotiate. A closer collaboration with universities could help in the latter respect.

Building a Framework of Key Elements of AI and Cyber Security for Emerging Economies

Based on the importance and interrelationships between AI and cyber security for emerging economies, governments in these economies could support firms in managing the transition from innovating in relation to traditional industrialization processes, in which mainly manual workers are employed, toward innovating in the knowledge economy, in which knowledge workers; that is, individuals with graduate-level abilities regarding critical thinking, technology and communication are employed. In particular, we suggest a focus on the following areas in which governments of emerging economies could facilitate the development of AI and cyber security knowledge workers (Figure 1, based on Strusani and Houngbonon (2019) and Heinl (2014)).

In Figure 1, we present our conceptual model, in which AI advantages, including focal areas of cyber security regarding AI, impact a number of economic factors. Simultaneously, various elements such as human capital development, simplified access to credit and innovative products and business models drive growth and development of the knowledge economy. In turn, these factors can positively influence the overall economic performance of an emerging economy. In particular, AI can be beneficial when it is used in combination with online courses by making education affordable, thus raising learning and employment in emerging economies. Similarly, via automation, AI enables substantial cost reductions of all key business processes, i.e. operations, marketing, human resources and accounting. For example, employee recruitment often means the costly review of numerous candidate profiles. AI can automate this process (Strusani & Houngbonon, 2019).

According to Heinl (2014), the cyber security focal areas shown in Figure 1 can also greatly benefit from AI applications, as these focal areas can be automated using AI technologies. The rationale for this is that pre-fixed automation designs are often inferior to AI automation designs.

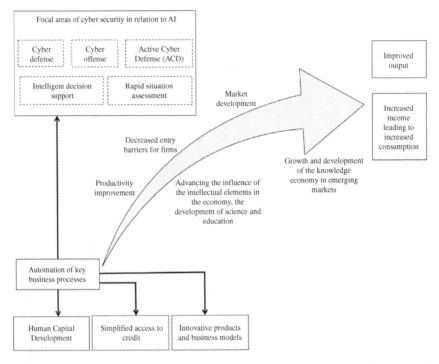

Figure 1. AI and cyber security facilitating the knowledge economy in emerging economies

In particular, new exposures, exploits and outages can happen concurrently (i.e. cyber defense, cyber offense, and rapid situation assessment). Individuals seem to experience difficulties in handling such exposures due to the large volumes of data and the speed of processes, if solutions are not highly automated (Beaudoin *et al.*, 2009). Thus, events can only be analyzed with delays without any intelligent decision support, which means that effective decision-making regarding any cyber-attacks is also unnecessarily delayed (Tyugu, 2011). Finally, Active Cyber Defense (ACD) is about the launch of proactive measures that defend against malicious cyber activities. Specifically, ACD can respond to a cyber-attack via detection and forensics, deception, as well as attack termination (Heinl, 2014).

Despite these advantages, in order for these AI automation designs to deliver the promised impact in relation to cyber security, a number of legal consequences, ideological and ethical issues, public perception concerns, public–private sector implications and economic aspects have to be addressed. Despite these concerns, AI applications are envisaged to deliver superior solutions to the cyber security focal areas highlighted in Figure 1 (Heinl, 2014). Automation of key business process such as access to credit (Figure 1) offer financial service benefits as data can be processed more effectively and more efficiently, allowing for improved access to credit. In addition, information asymmetries between lenders and borrowers of funds can be reduced, again, enabling better access to money.

Finally, AI can also facilitate the development of innovative products and business models. In particular, this can happen in the transportation and logistics industries, where firms in emerging economies often lack the ability to turn unstructured data into meaningful structured data, allowing for improvements in products and services. The above AI advantages and the AI advantages in relation to cyber security enable improvements of economic factors, such as productivity, entry barriers and market development. These advantages ultimately influence economic performance concerning overall economic outputs, consumption and income (Strusani & Houngbonon, 2019). Emerging economies could emulate AI and cyber security innovations prevalent in modern economies, which are relevant to their main industrial set up as opposed to starting broad-scale innovation efforts in these areas from a clean slate. In this way, emerging economies have an opportunity to develop their own knowledge economies, enabling them to enhance creativity and innovation, while simultaneously being able to protect critical infrastructures.

Conclusion

In this chapter, we discussed the influence and recent developments of AI and cyber security on emerging economies. We build a framework of key elements of AI and cyber security that would positively influence the knowledge economy of developing countries, leading to improved outputs as well as increased income and consumption. For future research, we intend to explore the uncertainty surrounding the future shaping of AI tools and techniques, in particular intelligent agents and disruptive technology that combine other disciplines. The policy implications for developing economies are multi-fold, for example the rise of legal issues around AI and cyber security, ideological and ethical concerns, public perception, impact on workforce and economic issues. These policy gaps require immediate attention and solutions that take into consideration the rapidly evolving landscape of AI and cyber security.

References

Antonescu, M. & Birău, R. (2015). Financial and non-financial implications of cybercrimes in emerging countries. *Procedia Economics and Finance, 32*, 618–621.

Asheim, B. & Gertler, M. (2006). The geography of innovation: Regional innovation systems. In: J. Fegerberg, D. C. Mowery and R. R. Nelson (eds.), *The Oxford Handbook of Innovation*. Oxford: Oxford University Press, pp. 291–317.

Baker, E.W. (2014). A model for the impact of cybersecurity infrastructure on economic development in emerging economies: evaluating the contrasting cases of India and Pakistan. *Information Technology for Development, 20*(2), 122–139.

Beaudoin, L., Japkowicz, N. & Matwin, S. (2009). Autonomic computer network defence using risk state and reinforcement learning. *Cryptology and Information Security Series, 3*, 238–248.

Brinkley, I. (2006). *Defining the knowledge economy*. Retrieved from: http://www.observatorioabaco.es/biblioteca/docs/98_TWF_2006.pdf.

Castellacci, F. (2015). Business groups, innovation, and market development in Latin America. *World Development, 70*, 43–58.

Chowdhry, A. (2018). Artificial Intelligence to Create 58 Million New Jobs by 2022. Retrieved from: https://www.forbes.com/sites/amitchowdhry/2018/09/18/artificialintelligence-to-create-58-million-new-jobs-by-2022-says-report/-2b45f6144d4b.

Clemente, D. (2013). Cyber security and global interdependence: What is critical? Chatham House, Royal Institute of International Affairs.

Crabtree, J. (2018). Robots threaten Asian jobs. *Nikkei Asian Review.* Retrieved from: https://asia.nikkei.com/Opinion/Robots-threaten-Asian-jobs2 [Accessed on November 3, 2019].

Craigen, D., Diakun-Thibault, N. & Purse, R. (2014). Defining cybersecurity. *Technology Innovation Management Review, 4*(10), 13–21.

Crossan, M. & Apaydin, M. (2010). A multi-dimensional framework of organizational innovation: A systematic review of the literature. *Journal of Management Studies, 47*(6), 1154–1191.

Dalenogare, L.S., Benitez, G.B., Ayala, N.F. & Frank, A.G. (2018). The expected contribution of Industry 4.0 technologies for industrial performance. *International Journal of Production Economics, 204*, 383–394.

Dimitratos, P., Amoros, E., Etchebarne, S. & Felzensztein, C. (2014). Micromultinational or not? The effect of international entrepreneurship, networking and learning. *Journal of Business Research*, 67(5), 908–915.

Diniz, G., Muggah, R. & Glenny, M. (2014). *Deconstructing cyber security in Brazil: Threats and Responses*. Retrieved from: https://igarape.org.br/wp-content/uploads/2014/11/Strategic-Paper-11-Cyber2.pdf.

Gordon, R.J. (2000). Does the" new economy" measure up to the great inventions of the past? *Journal of Economic Perspectives*, 14(4), 49–74.

Gosler, J.R. & Von Thaer, L. (2013). *Task Force Report: Resilient Military Systems and the Advanced Cyber Threat*. Washington, DC: Department of Defense, Defense Science Board, p. 41.

Green, D. (2017). What does Artificial Intelligence mean for the future of poor countries? Retrieved from: https://oxfamblogs.org/fp2p/what-does-artificial-intelligence-mean-for-the-future-of-poor-countries/.

Hall, B. & Rosenberg, N. (2010). The handbook of economics of innovation. In: B. Hall and N. Rosenberg (eds.), *The Handbook of Economics of Innovation*, Vol. 1. Amsterdam: North-Holland Publications: Elsevier, pp. 3–9.

Harknett, R.J. & Stever, J.A. (2009). The cybersecurity triad: Government, private sector partners, and the engaged cybersecurity citizen. *Journal of Homeland Security and Emergency Management*, 6(1), Article 79.

Heinl, C.H. (2014). Artificial (intelligent) agents and active cyber defence: Policy implications. Paper presented at the *2014 6th International Conference on Cyber Conflict (CyCon 2014)*.

Hoskisson, R.E., Eden, L., Lau, C.M. & Wright, M. (2000). Strategy in emerging economies. *Academy of Management Journal*, 43(3), 249–267.

ITU. (2019). The Global Cybersecurity Index (GCI). Retrieved from: https://www.itu.int/en/ITU-D/Cybersecurity/Documents/draft-18-00706_Global-Cybersecurity-Index-EV5_print_2.pdf.

Kalyanakrishnan, S., Panicker, R.A., Natarajan, S. & Rao, S. (2018). Opportunities and Challenges for Artificial Intelligence in India. Paper presented at the *Proceedings of the 2018 AAAI/ACM Conference on AI, Ethics, and Society*.

KPMG. (2016). Cybersecurity in China. Retrieved from: https://assets.kpmg/content/dam/kpmg/cn/pdf/en/2016/08/cyber-security-in-china.pdf

Leung, R. (2018). Can Artificial Intelligence Propel Emerging Markets? Retrieved from: https://emerge85.io/Insights/can-artificialintelligence-propel-emerging-markets/.

Levitt, T. (1983). The globalization of markets. *Harvard Business Review*, 61(May–June), 92–102.

Liu, H., Hou, J., Yang, P. & Ding, X.H. (2011). Entrepreneurial orientation, organizational capability, and competitive advantage in emerging economies: Evidence from China. *African Journal of Business Management*, 5(10), 3891.

Machlup, F. (1962). *The Production and Distribution of Knowledge in the United States*, Vol. 278. Princeton: Princeton University Press.

MGI. (2017). Reinventing construction: A route to higher productivity. Retrieved from: https://www.mckinsey.com/~/media/McKinsey/Industries/Capital Projects and Infrastructure/Our Insights/Reinventing construction through a productivity revolution/MGI-Reinventing-Construction-Executive-summary. ashx.

Mooi, R. & Botha, R.A. (2016). Prioritizing computer security incident response services for the South African National Research Network (SANReN). Paper presented at the CONF-IRM.

Muller Jr, D.G. (2009). Improving futures intelligence. *International Journal of Intelligence and CounterIntelligence*, 22(3), 382–395.

Nabi, K. (2019). The Impact of Artificial Intelligence (AI) on Workforce in Emerging Economies. *Global Journal of Management And Business Research*, 19(8), 50–59. Retrieved from: https://journalofbusiness.org/index.php/GJMBR/article/view/2802.

Nonaka, I. & Takeuchi, H. (1995). *The Knowledge Creating Company: How Japanese Companies Foster Creativity and Innovation for Competitive Advantage*. New York: Oxford University Press.

OECD. (2019). Business insights on emerging markets 2019. Retrieved from: https://www.oecd.org/dev/BI_2019.pdf.

Powell, W.W. & Snellman, K. (2004). The knowledge economy. *Annual Review of Sociology*, 30, 199–220.

Rasheed, A. (2018). Artificial Intelligence and the future of work. *Dhaka Tribune*. Retrieved from: https://www.dhakatribune.com/business/2018/05/30/artificial-intelligence-and-the-future-of-work.

Singer, P.W. & Friedman, A. (2014). *Cybersecurity: What Everyone Needs to Know*. USA: OUP USA.

Strusani, D. & Houngbonon, G.V. (2019). The role of artificial intelligence in supporting development in emerging markets. Retrieved from: http://documents.worldbank.org/curated/en/539371567673606214/The-Role-of-Artificial-Intelligence-in-Supporting-Development-in-Emerging-Markets.

Sukharenko, A. (2019). Russian ITC security policy and cybercrime. Retrieved from: http://www.ponarseurasia.org/memo/russian-itc-security-policy-and-cybercrime.

Tagert, A.C. (2010). *Cybersecurity Challenges in Developing Nations*. Figshare.

Tyugu, E. (2011). Artificial intelligence in cyber defense. Paper presented at the *2011 3rd International Conference on Cyber Conflict*, Tallinn, Estonia.

Webb, J.W., Bruton, G.D., Tihanyi, L. & Ireland, R.D. (2013). Research on entrepreneurship in the informal economy: Framing a research agenda. *Journal of Business Venturing*, 28(5), 598–614.

Yusuf, S. (2017). Automation, AI, and the emerging economies. Retrieved from: https://www.cgdev.org/publication/automation-aiand-emerging-economies.

Zhang, S., Song, S., Yang, F., Li, R., Zhao, Z. & Zhang, H. (2019). *The* design and implementation of intelligent software defined security framework. Paper presented at *The 25th Annual International Conference on Mobile Computing and Networking.*

Chapter 5

Predicting Poverty Rates with Consumer Survey Results: A MIDAS Approach

Mirjana Čižmešija and Tihana Škrinjarić[*]

University of Zagreb, Croatia

[*]tskrinjar@net.efzg.hr

Consumer surveys (CSs) conducted in accordance with *The Joint Harmonized European Union Program of Business and Consumer Surveys* produce very useful data for economic modeling and forecasting, especially within the area of macroeconomic and financial applications. One part of the application is the investigation of poverty levels and social problems. Therefore, the purpose of this chapter is to examine if the monthly data available from CS can be used to forecast future poverty rates of a country. This research utilizes the mixed sampling (MIDAS) regression approach of modeling and forecasting the yearly poverty rates of a country by using monthly data on the financial situation from the CS data. Results of the analysis show that the potential of using such an approach exists. This means that policymakers of emerging markets could use the MIDAS regression to forecast future poverty rates so that timely decisions and moves can be made, which will reduce costs and achieve the country's goals of better and faster development.

Introduction

The challenge of this research is investigating the possibilities of applying the *Harmonized EU Consumer Survey* (CS) results in tracking and forecasting poverty levels by applying the MIDAS (mixed sampling data) regression approach. How to use CS data in that? Are there any benefits in using CS data? Namely, as a complement to the annual *EU Statistics on Income and Living Conditions* (EU-SILC) variables, CS offers a considerable benefit by providing monthly information on the consumers' financial position. Reasoning on why such an approach should be made can be found in the UN (2015) consensus that in order to follow policy goals and reduce poverty, the whole procedure requires a measurement of poverty. The recent crisis and recession in Europe which started in 2008 actualizes the problem of poverty and all other social problems (Nikoloski, 2010; Rewilak, 2018). The announcements (*The Guardian*, 2019; ECB, 2019) of a new one in the next few years highlights it. So, the scientific and professional community continually deals with different aspects and consequences of poverty and financial problems with the possibilities to use more frequent and reliable data sources valuable for tracking and predicting poverty levels in EU countries and in the EU as a whole. Using EU-SILC data has the main limitation presented through the short time series and their yearly frequency. Based on the standard EU-SILC indicators, the two main goals of the research in our work are as follows: the construction of a new composite CS indicator and using a new SC indicator and several individual CS variables as proxies for some EU-SILC indicators using a relatively new methodological approach in this field of interest presented as the MIDAS regression for the prediction poverty rates. It has been shown previously that data from CS provide information about future consumer consumption (Bram & Ludvigson, 1998; Ludvigson, 2004). The main research hypothesis is that possibilities exist in complementing the predictive power of EU-SILC data with the addition of the CS data related to the poverty level in MIDAS regression models. The relatively new methodological approach presented in this work produces the composite indicator, calculated in accordance with the standard EU procedure in estimating the economic sentiment indicator (ESI). The new CS indicator is based on monthly CS data. It could serve as a timely indicator of cumulous socio-economic problems in EU countries and, in that way, it can significantly complement the EU-SILC data. Three CS variables used separately in analyses have a similar mission: namely, the harmonized

European CS offers three questions pointing to the financial situation of households (Q1: financial situation over the last 12 months, Q2: financial situation over the next 12 months and Q3: statement on the financial situation of household). These questions have a monthly frequency, so they provide more detailed information about the prevailing social trends than the annual EU-SILC data. The next part of the research is the application of the mixed sampling (MIDAS) regression approach in modeling and forecasting the yearly poverty rates of a country by using monthly CS data, as a relatively new survey method in this kind of research. The empirical analysis is made on a country in transition, namely Croatia, by observing the time period from 2010 to 2018. CS is a widely used data source. The main advantage of such data is that the results of these surveys can be numerically expressed, simply presented and then summarized into composite indicators of varying degrees of aggregation with certain predictive properties. As such, they are available to a wide range of users, often well before the same official statistics are available. In addition, the indicators derived from these surveys present the macroeconomic phenomena through a different dimension than that provided by official statistics. Official statistics show changes in objective conditions, and CS show consumers' attitude to them through subjective ratings and expectations. It is particularly important to emphasize that the harmonization of the methodology of conducting CS has enabled comparability of results across EU countries (Čižmešija *et al.*, 2018).

Despite the primarily subjective character of the data obtained from CS, it has been empirically confirmed that indicators derived from the survey have the characteristics of matching or even preceding indicators to selected reference macroeconomic variables and can be used as such in interpreting and predicting macroeconomic variables, whose actual values are often only recorded on an annual basis and are not immediately available, like EU-SILC data. Results of applying the MIDAS regression approach presented in this work confirmed this conclusion. The main contributions of this study include the following: to the knowledge of the authors, this is a first attempt in utilizing the MIDAS approach in modeling yearly poverty rates based on the CS monthly data. Previous literature uses the same frequencies of data in order to obtain future forecasts, which lag more compared to the results obtained in this study. Managerial and policy implications based on the obtained results include using such an approach in obtaining the future forecasts of poverty rates in a way that is quicker and much less costly compared to the official international institutions approach. This could save money and time in future research and decision-making. These are significant findings for policymakers that aim to reduce poverty and inequality of a country, which is especially important for developing and emerging markets. The rest of the chapter describes the usefulness of using CS variables in econometric modeling, and the description of the applied methodology, with detailed empirical analysis. The final part of the chapter gives the discussion and conclusion.

Consumer Survey and EU-SICL

CS is a part of harmonized EU Business and Consumer surveys (BCSs), harmonized and unified on the EU level. This survey is conducted on a monthly level. The European Commission has defined *The Joint Harmonized EU Programme of Business and Consumer Surveys*, to fully synchronize BCS on the EU level. This program was launched by the European Commission decision of 15 November 1961, and it is continuously updated and modified through the Council and Commission decisions. CS was included in The Joint Harmonized EU Program in 1972. CS deals with consumers' assessments, explanations and expectations of key economic variables like the consumers' financial situation, general economic situation, consumer prices, unemployment, major purchases of durable consumer goods, savings and savings intentions (European Commission, 2019a). The CS questionnaire has 12 monthly questions and three quarterly questions. The sample units are consumers, usually chosen in the stratified sample with a random choice. The answers in CS have four, five or six options. Answers obtained from the survey are aggregated in the form of *balance*. Balance is a difference between the percentage of respondents giving positive and negative answers (European Commission, 2019a). If questions have six alternative options (most useful in CS) — positive (up, more, more than sufficient, good, to large, increase, improve, etc.), neutral (unchanged, as much, sufficient, satisfactory, adequate, etc.) and negative (down, less, not sufficient, too small, decline, etc.), with the addition of very positive (very much higher, increase sharply, etc.), very negative (very unfavorable, fall sharply, etc.) and don't know — then the balance is calculated as a weighted average. If P, N and M denote the percentage of respondents having chosen options positive, neutral and negative, respectively, then PP denotes the percentage of respondents having chosen the option "very positive" and MM the percentage of respondents having chosen the option "very negative" (PP + P + E + M + MM + N = 100), and the balance is calculated as B = (PP + ½P) − (½M + MM). After that, balances have to be seasonally adjusted (for all variables of interest in the survey) and used to calculate the composite confidence indicators. The time series of seasonally adjusted balances for all variables (questions) in the survey can be used in empirical analyses. The use of composite indicators was shown as much more useful and usable. Variable components of indicators are chosen in accordance with *The Joint Harmonized EU Programme of Business and Consumer Surveys*, so the confidence indicators are calculated using the unique methodology in EU members. The choice of variables in indicators was conducted with the aim of achieving coincident correlation, as high as possible, of the confidence indicator with a reference series. The main goal of CS is to collect information on households' spending and savings intentions and to assess their perception of the factors influencing these decisions (Kurnoga and Čižmešija, 2016). Thus, the Consumer Confidence Indicator (CCI) includes four variables (derived from CS): the financial situation of households, the general economic situation, unemployment expectations (with an inverted sign) and savings, all over the next 12 months (European Commission, 2019a). In addition to the standard CCI indicator, CS variables can be used to calculate some other new indicators.

On the contrary, the EU-SILC data cover the multidimensional datasets, presented as a list of policy indicators (income and living conditions: people at risk of poverty or social exclusion, income distribution and monetary poverty, living conditions and material deprivation). EU-SILC data have been published recently. In 2003, following the Eurostat initiation, six EU member states (Austria, Belgium, Denmark, Greece, Ireland and Luxembourg) and Norway have established the EU-SILC project, with the aim to quantify the poverty levels and social problems in individual EU countries. EU-SILC project started in 2004 in EU-15 (except in Germany, the Netherlands and the United Kingdom), in Estonia, Norway and Iceland. Since 2005, the new EU-SILC covers EU member states and several non-EU countries (Eurostat, 2006). The main limitations in international comparability of EU-SILC datasets are different data collection approaches across countries. One of the major differences is that some countries rely entirely on household surveys, while others also use administrative or "register" data (Lohman, 2011). Nevertheless, many empirical studies are based on EU-SILC data (Ayllón and Gábos, 2017; Čižmešija *et al.*, 2018; Guagnano *et al.*, 2016; Krell *et al.*, 2017; Rastrigina *et al.*, 2015). It is indisputable that the EU-SILC produce important variables related to the general national poverty levels, but due to their annual frequencies and limited international comparability, they need to be supplemented with new datasets. It is especially important in a period of recession like the last one to have occurred in 2008; namely, monthly data may be used to promptly signalize a change of variables in a timely manner. Just the CS monthly data are a great complement to the EU-SILC. Additionally, CS data are fully harmonized at the EU level. The variables of interest in CS can be the financial situation of a household over the last 12 months, expected financial position of a household over the next 12 months and current financial situation of households (as we will explain in the rest of the chapter). All of those three variables (their balances) can be used in tracking and predicting the poverty rate. The next step is the calculation of a composite indicator of poverty, based on standard EU methodology for calculating ESI. With this in mind, this research aims to assess the value of CS responses to households' financial distress. This is expressed as a new monthly, inter-EU comparable, indicator by correlating them to the common measures of poverty in Croatia.

Literature Review

Recently, in the last 10 years, the need has been noted to develop a system of new indicators and improve the database needed for empirical research in tracking and forecasting the poverty level. The approach to measuring poverty so far has been based solely on income, but due to the multidimensionality of this phenomenon, it is necessary to improve the approach to poverty measurement (Čižmešija *et al.*, 2018). Poverty is determined by social exclusion and a range of socio-economic characteristics of households and individuals (Whelan *et al.*, 2014). Just the need for a multidimensional measure of poverty and its multidimensionality open up the possibility and opportunity to include CS data in this field of poverty measures. Navicke *et al.* (2014) highlighted the importance of the at-risk-of-poverty rate as a measure in monitoring the progress of the implementation of the Europe 2020 strategy to reduce poverty and social exclusion. It is where EU-SILC yearly data can be supplemented with other data sources with monthly frequencies. Specifically, due to the complex nature of the EU-SILC, a poverty risk assessment is published with a delay of 2–3 years. As a timely publication of this indicator is crucial for monitoring policy effectiveness, any step forward in producing equivalent indicators, which are available much earlier than EU-SILC data, is more than welcome. In doing so, many authors (mentioned below) supplemented the unavailable data by estimating the at-risk-of-poverty rate based on tax relief and income data combined with selected macroeconomic variables. Corluy and Vandrbroucke (2017) investigated the relationship between employment and social inclusion policies of individuals and households in EU countries. The research was based on data from the EU Labor Force Surveys (EU-LFS, The European Union Labor Force Survey) and the EU-SILC. Changes in the at-risk-of-poverty rates were monitored, based on changes in the at-risk-of-poverty households with no job, changes in household unemployment due to changes in individual employment rates and changes in household structures and based on changes in the distribution of employment. The research was conducted to identify and explain the link between employment and social inclusion policies. The main limitation of the research is the lack of an up-to-date data source and the need to find alternative data sources. This is one of the research segments that opens the space for the inclusion of CS data. The first formal attempt to examine the ability of CS results in an empirical survey with the aim to forecast household spending within a multicounty framework using CS data was made by Cotsomitis and Kwan (2006). However, this research, together with others which followed afterward, uses (mostly) monthly data within vector auto regression (VAR) models to estimate relationships between spending and consumer sentiment. Thus, all of the used variables are often on a monthly basis. The MIDAS regression methodology approach has, to the knowledge of the authors, not yet been applied to the consumer sentiment data in such a fashion as it is applied in this research. Data that are often delayed in public announcements and used in tailoring macroeconomic policies, to the knowledge of the authors, have not yet been modeled in such a fashion that the analysis provides future values in advance.

Methodology

The CS Composite Indicator of Households' Financial Distress (CSI2)

The three questions of interest in CS used in the calculation of the CS composite indicator of households' financial distress are as follows: (1) How has the financial situation of your household changed over the last 12 months? It has ++, got a lot better; +, got a little better; =, stayed the same; −, got a little worse; − −, got a lot worse, N, don't know. (2) How do you expect the financial position of your household to change over the next 12 months? It will ++, get a lot better; +, get a little better; =, stay the same; −, get a little worse; − −, get a lot worse; and N, don't know. (3) Which of these statements best describes the current financial situation of your household? ++, we are saving a lot; +, we are saving a little; =, we are just managing to make ends meet on our income; −, we are having to draw on our savings; − −, we are running into debt; and N, don't know.

Following the EU harmonized methodology of calculating the composite indicator ESI (with minor modifications), the CS composite indicator of households' financial distress (CSI2) was calculated as follows. Three variables (x_j) are used (as indicated above) — Q1: financial situation over the last 12 months, Q2: financial situation over the next 12 months and Q12: statement on the financial situation of household (denoted as x_j, $j = 1, 2, 3$). All three variables of the indicator component are treated as equally significant in its calculation, and therefore, the weighting procedure was not necessary. Each individual variable is standardized (y_j). The standardization is conducted over a frozen sample to avoid monthly revisions of the index, as in Equations (1) and (2), as follows:

$$y_{j,t} = \frac{x_{j,t} - \overline{x}_j}{s_j}; \ \forall j = 1,2,3; \ t = 1,2,\ldots,n, \tag{1}$$

$$\overline{x}_j = \frac{1}{T'}\sum_{t=1}^{T'} x_{j,t}; \ s_j = \sqrt{\frac{1}{T'-1}\sum_{t=1}^{T'}(x_{j,t} - \overline{x}_j)^2}, \tag{2}$$

where T' denotes the number of observations in the frozen sample (period) and is defined for the period from January 2006 to December 2016, thus $T' = 80$. The weighted average z_t of the individual standardized response balances is then calculated, as in Equation (3), as follows:

$$z_t = \frac{\sum_{j=1}^{3} y_{j,t}}{3}; \ t = 1,2,\ldots,n. \tag{3}$$

The weighted average z_t is then scaled to have a long-term mean of 100 and a standard deviation of 10, as in Equations (4) and in (5), as follows:

$$\text{CSI2}_t = \left(\frac{z_t - \overline{z}}{s_z} \right) \cdot 10 + 100; \quad t = 1, 2, \ldots, n, \tag{4}$$

$$\overline{z} = \frac{1}{T'} \sum_{t=1}^{T'} z_t, \quad s_z = \sqrt{\frac{1}{T'-1} \sum_{t=1}^{T'} (z_t - \overline{z})^2}. \tag{5}$$

The interpretation of CSI2 is as follows: if the value of CSI2 is equal to 100, it is concluded that consumer sentiment related to the household financial situation is above average. The value of CSI2 less than 100 indicates that the consumer sentiment is at a below average level.

MIDAS Regression Approach

Modeling and forecasting lower frequency data by using higher frequency ones is often done by using the MIDAS (mixed data sampling) regression. This is evident in macroeconomic forecasting of variables that usually become available with a great time lag, like the GDP and its components. The most recent contributions include those by Clements and Galvao (2008, 2009), Andreou *et al.* (2013), Duarte (2014), Foroni *et al.* (2015), etc. It is assumed we have a low-frequency variable y_t (e.g. yearly data), which we want to model and forecast by using a high-frequency variable $x_\tau^{(m)}$, where τ is the period for the high-frequency variable and t is the period for the low-frequency variable and m denotes the number of times the high-frequency variable appears in the same basic unit t of the low-frequency dependent variable. The basic MIDAS regression that we will be utilizing in the chapter is the following one:

$$y_t = \beta_0 + \beta_1 B(L^{\frac{1}{m}}; \theta) x_\tau^{(m)} + \varepsilon_t, \tag{6}$$

where $B(L^{\frac{1}{m}}; \theta)$ is the high-frequency lag polynomial, defined as

$$B(L^{\frac{1}{m}}; \theta) = \sum_{k=0}^{K} b(k; \theta) L^{\frac{k}{m}}, \tag{7}$$

with k denoting the high-frequency variable lags and $b(k;\theta)$ denoting the functional form of the polynomial, with parameter θ. The researcher needs to define which functional form will be utilized in order to estimate

Equation (6) by including Equation (7) by choosing a parsimonious approach, due to reducing the number of the parameters that need to be estimated for the high-frequency variable. The commonly used functions are the following ones: beta function (Ghysels *et al.*, 2004, 2005, 2006a, 2006b):

$$b(k;\theta_1,\theta_2) = \frac{f\left(\frac{k}{m},\theta_1,\theta_2\right)}{\sum_{j=1}^{m} f\left(\frac{j}{m},\theta_1,\theta_2\right)}, \tag{8}$$

and the exponential Almon specification (Ghysels *et al.*, 2005, 2007):

$$b(k;\theta_1,\theta_2) = \frac{\exp(\theta_1 k + \theta_2 k^2)}{\sum_{j=1}^{m} \exp(\theta_1 k + \theta_2 k^2)}. \tag{9}$$

The Almon specification in Equation (9) is a popular specification, whereas the general form of this function is given as follows:

$$b(k;\theta) = \frac{\exp(\theta_1 k + \theta_2 k^2 + \cdots + \theta_q k^q)}{\sum_{j=1}^{m} \exp(\theta_1 k + \theta_2 k^2 + \cdots + \theta_q k^q)}, \tag{10}$$

where qs are shape parameters that determine the shape of the function b in (10). However, using the function in Equation (9) enables many different effects of lagged high-frequency data by using only two shape parameters. In essence, expression in Equation (9), i.e. Equation (10) are weights that are given to the lagged values of high-frequency variable x. If the model in (6) was extended to multiple independent variables, each high-frequency variable on the right-hand side could be of different frequency (i.e. a mix of daily, weekly, monthly, etc. data) and every variable could have its own specification of the function b. Function in Equation (10) could be observed as an aggregating function that will transform the high-frequency data into the low-frequency data of the dependent variable. The researcher can define the type of aggregation: it could be based on the lags of the high-frequency data, the independent variable which is being observed, on both, neither, etc. Thus, great flexibility is present in such modeling. The estimation of MIDAS models is done via ordinary least squares (OLS) if unrestricted MIDAS is estimated (without any restrictions on the parameters, see Foroni *et al.*, 2015). When we impose restrictions on the parameters (any of the functional forms for $B(L^{1/m};\theta)$), nonlinear least squares (NLS) are used. The usual assumptions on the error terms as in the ordinary regression have to hold (Gauss–Markov assumptions; i.e. normality, no autocorrelation and homoscedasticity of the error term). When using the NLS method, optimal values will be obtained as an iterative process, where the criterion for convergence has to be fulfilled: the sum of squares cannot decrease from one iteration to the next, where the difference is defined by the researcher. Many algorithms exist on how to search the optimal value (Gauss–Newton, the QR decomposition, Nelder–Mead algorithm). Details can be found in Kelley (1999) or Strutz (2016). Thus, the convergence test has to be performed if the stopping criterion is satisfied. This can be done by observing the gradient and the Hessian within the NLS problem (necessary and sufficient conditions of the convergence). A formal test can be conducted in which the Euclidian norm of the gradient is tested to be close to zero as well as the eigenvalues of the Hessian being positive.

Some of the weaknesses of this approach include the following. An optimal number of lags has to be chosen so that the model is parsimonious but has a good overall fit. This could represent a problem with empirical data. Furthermore, enough high-frequency data have to be available for this approach of modeling. Some of the usual goodness of fit measures cannot be applied to this semi-parametric approach. For more details, see Ghysels *et al.* (2019). Moreover, the test of the adequacy of chosen functional forms has to be performed, in which the parameters of the OLS estimation of the unrestricted MIDAS model are compared to the restricting ones. Details on the test and its HAC robust version (heteroscedasticity and autocorrelation consistent) can be found in Kvedaras and Zemlys (2012, 2013). Finally, when the researcher is not certain on how many lags of high-frequency data should be included in the model, the usual information criteria can be calculated and the model with the lowest values of the information criteria is chosen. MIDAS with a step functions approach is also available for empirical estimations, as the previously described methodology is a nonlinear one. Details on the methodology of the step functions MIDAS can be found in Ghysels *et al.* (2006b). However, since this approach is less parsimonious, it could be applied to a larger dataset (something which is not the case here). This approach does result in a simpler specification of the original model, so the interested readers could see more in Forsberg and Ghysels (2007). For more details on the MIDAS regression, refer to Andreou *et al.* (2010 a, b), Arouba *et al.* (2009), Ghysels *et al.* (2002, 2003, 2004, 2005, 2006a, 2006b, 2016) and Ghysels and Valkanov (2012).

Analyses

Data Description

For the purpose of the empirical analysis, we obtained yearly data on the risk of poverty rate cutoff point (60% of median equivalized income after social transfers) for Croatia in the available period: 2010–2018, from the website of the European Commission (2019b) and Eurostat (2019). From the European Commission website, monthly data for the same period were obtained for the CS questions Q1, Q2 and Q12. The variable CSI2 was constructed as described in the previous section. We divide the total sample into the in-sample estimation part (2010–2017) and the year 2018 was used for out-of-sample forecasts to determine the quality of the model. Since we are dealing with 8 yearly observations for the poverty variable, each CS question and the CSI2 variable are used individually to model the poverty rate. Thus, we compare four different models in the next subsection. Since the variables have to be stationary, as in the ordinary regression approach, to model them via the MIDAS regression, the monthly variables were tested via the augmented Dickey–Fuller (ADF) test. All of the monthly variables were found to be non-stationary on usual levels of significance. Thus, we differenced the monthly values and obtained stationary data, which we use in the regression modeling.

Results

For the in-sample estimation, the first 8 years of data were used to estimate the model; that is, from January 2010 to December 2017. Estimation of the MIDAS regressions was done with the assumption of the exponential Almon lag function (see Equation (9)), by changing the lag length k of the high-frequency variable ranging from one to five. Each of the high-frequency variables (Q1, Q2, Q12 and CSI2) has been used as a separate regressor in Equation (6). Thus, five models for each variable have been estimated. The usual assumptions about the error term within the regression model have been tested (such as the heteroscedasticity, etc.), and we found no problems (detailed results are available upon request). The Akaike and Schwartz information criteria (AIC and BIC, respectively) have been used to compare those models for different lag lengths.

Detailed results are shown in Table 1. Column labeled "variable" denotes the variable that has been included as the explanatory one to forecast the yearly at-risk-of-poverty rate. Column "lag" gives information about how many high-frequency lags have been included in the model. AIC and BIC are the aforementioned information criteria, with notation

Table 1.   Comparison of MIDAS regressions for every explanatory variable

Variable	Lag	AIC r	BIC r	AIC u	BIC u	Restriction test p-value	Convergence
Q1	1	19.44	19.76	19.44	19.76	0.00	0
	2	20.23	20.55	21.27	21.67	0.47	0
	3	19.39	19.71	22.75	23.22	0.88	0
	4	**12.67**	**12.99**	**16.41**	**16.96**	**0.88**	**0**
	5	17.98	18.30	12.39	13.02	0.66	1
Q2	1	19.15	19.47	19.15	19.47	1.00	0
	2	18.60	18.91	18.46	18.86	0.26	0
	3	**18.12**	**18.43**	**20.36**	**20.84**	**0.69**	**0**
	4	19.25	19.57	16.96	17.52	0.30	0
	5	19.31	19.63	11.51	12.14	0.18	0
Q12	1	20.19	20.51	20.08	20.40	1.00	0
	2	19.00	19.32	19.20	19.59	0.31	0
	3	**18.82**	**19.14**	**20.70**	**21.18**	**0.63**	**0**
	4	19.97	20.29	20.76	21.31	0.60	0
	5	20.10	20.42	22.71	23.34	0.91	0
CSI2	1	14.02	14.34	14.02	14.34	0.00	0
	2	15.44	15.76	10.11	10.51	0.01	0
	3	**15.47**	**15.78**	**9.19**	**9.67**	**0.02**	**0**
	4	15.45	15.77	11.08	11.63	0.15	0
	5	19.29	19.61	10.88	11.52	0.14	0

Notes: Values provided in bold indicate the best model for each variable. p-values refer to the test of the null hypothesis that the adequate functional constraint is used. Values 0 and 1 in the last column refer to achieving the convergence in the optimization procedure (value 0) or not (value 1). u and r refer to the unrestricted and restricted version of the estimated MIDAS model.

"r" for the restricted model and "u" for the unrestricted versions. Values provided in bold indicate the best value with respect to all of the lags included in the analysis, e.g. the variable Q1 used as the regressor has the best lag 4, due to minimal values of each criterion (AIC r and BIC r). The restriction test p-value column refers to the p-value of the test of adequacy of the restrictions in the specific model. The value of 0.884 for the fourth lag indicates that the null hypothesis of this test cannot be rejected as the p-value is greater than the usual levels of significance. Finally, the column "convergence" refers to the necessary and sufficient tests of convergence of the optimization algorithm. Value 1 indicates that no convergence has been obtained and that the model cannot be used. The fourth chosen lag for the Q1 variable has the best performance in terms of the mentioned information criteria, restriction test and due to it converging. As can be seen from the rest of Table 1, the optimal model was three lags for the rest of the variables (based on the information criteria). The restriction tests indicate that the null hypothesis cannot be rejected on the usual levels of significance for all of the Q variables and 1(%) for the CSI2 variable. Convergence is achieved in all of the models which have values provided in bold in Table 1. When comparing the values provided in bold of information criteria between the variables, it is evident that the smallest values are present for variable Q1. These results indicate that using the variable Q1 monthly with four monthly lags can be used to model and predict the yearly at-risk-of-poverty rate in Croatia. These are just statistical interpretations on using the best model with the best number of lags and the variable, which will enhance the modeling results in the best way measured via statistical measures.

In the next step, we utilize the estimated models from Table 1 to forecast the value of the poverty rate in Croatia for 2018 (out of sample forecast). The true value in 2018 was 19.4%, and the following values were obtained for all of the four models: 19.36%, 20.22%, 20.07% and 20.48% for the Q1, Q2, Q12 and CSI2 model, respectively. The first model produces forecast value closest to the true value. Moreover, we compared the in-sample estimates with the true value in Figure 1. Again, the model with the Q1 variable is the best, due to the differences between the true and estimated values being the smallest. This is confirmed in Table 2, where the forecast errors have been calculated for the entire observed period (in and out of sample). Thus, the variable Q1 could be used in future research as the most accurate variable on a monthly basis to predict the yearly values of the poverty rates in Croatia. As it is obvious from

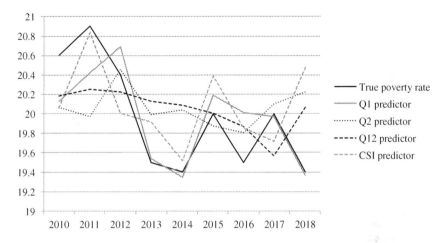

Figure 1. In sample estimates compared to true poverty rate values

Table 2. Forecast error comparisons of the estimated models

Error/predictor	Q1	Q2	Q12	CSI2
RMSE	0.306	0.537	0.501	0.490
MAE	0.234	0.444	0.448	0.404
MAPE	0.012	0.022	0.023	0.020

Note: RMSE, MAE and MAPE denote root mean-squared error, mean absolute error and mean absolute percentage error, respectively.

Table 2, the root mean-squared error, mean absolute error and mean absolute percentage errors are smallest for the variable Q1. These errors are calculated as the average deviations of the estimated values from the true values of the variable of interest. Regarding variable Q1, the interpretations are as follows: average deviation of the estimated values of the true poverty rate from the true values is equal to 0.306 percentage points, whereas the mean absolute deviation is equal to 0.23 percentage points (and in percentage, this is equal to 1.2% (MAPE)).

Discussion and Conclusion

With the aim to support and supplement the annual EU-SICL data on the poverty level with monthly CS data, three CS variables were considered.

Using these three variables, a new composite CSI2 indicator, as a measure of the poverty level is defined. The forecasting power for each individual variable and for the CSI2 was examined using the MIDAS regression approach. The main research hypothesis, about the existence of the possibility to improve the predictive power of EU-SILC data with the addition of the CS data related to the poverty level, was confirmed, based on Croatia's dataset. The main purpose of this chapter is to show that using monthly CS data on selected variables related to the financial situation of consumers could be used to model and forecast yearly data on the poverty rates. This was done by using the MIDAS regression approach, in which the monthly data were aggregated to yearly in the optimization process of estimating the model's parameters. In the case of Croatia as an observed country, the question (variable) Q1 (Financial situation over the last 12 months) was the best one to use as a predictor. Thus, future rates of poverty for this country could be forecasted by using the MIDAS approach and the Q1 monthly data. The importance of using such an approach of forecasting can be seen in obtaining the previously unavailable data on poverty rates before the official data will be published. In this way, policymakers could change the existing measures being used for specific purposes of reducing the inequalities within the society. This would reduce the total costs of providing quality policies to reduce poverty, as future values of relevant variables can be obtained in advance. Implications for managers interested in topics observed in this study include the following. First, in order to reduce the poverty within a country, a monitoring system that can quantify and accurately forecast the important variables needs to be constructed. However, the timing of such activities needs to be in accordance with the needs and limitations of the policymakers and managers involved in the process. This is why this study has focused on the methodological aspect of obtaining the results more quickly compared to the usual approaches of annual surveys and indices construction which provide data with great lags. By using the MIDAS approach in modeling, policymakers can make timely decisions when the national budget is being set, without delays. Furthermore, using the data this study has utilized is less costly compared to obtaining data from specialized institutions. The data used here were freely available, which is another advantage of using such an approach. By observing the findings in the empirical section, the forecasting of the future risk of poverty can be based on the Q1 question. (*How has the financial situation of your household changed over the last 12 months?*) Since the answers to this question are available on a monthly basis, policymakers can track them throughout the entire year. If some particular changes occur within the answers, measures of the economic policy targeting poverty and its reduction can be modified on time, and not with great lags. Some of the shortfalls of this study include a relatively short time span of data that was available for the study. That is why future work should extend the observed period when new data become available. Furthermore, only SC data were used in the study as the regressor, whereas other micro and macro variables should be included in future work as well. Here, it was not possible to include them due to the small amount of data available for the dependent variable, which reduced the degrees of freedom in the model. Such analysis can be done in future research on other similar countries, especially those which are classified as the emerging markets. In that way, the CS data can have one more useful purpose, among many others. Future research should include a longer data time span, to check for the robustness of the results obtained here. Moreover, each country analysis should individually look at which specific CS question is the most useful in forecasting yearly poverty rates. In the future, when the data on such issues will be richer, other variables could be considered within the model to see if the forecasting abilities will enhance when controlling for other variables as well.

References

Andreou, E., Ghysels, E. & Kourtellos, A. (2010a). Should macroeconomic forecasters use daily financial data and how? Working paper. Retrieved from: http,//w4.stern.nyu.edu/emplibrary/Macro_MIDAS_Feb_22_2010_CEPR.pdf [Accessed on August 30, 2019].

Andreou, E., Ghysels, E. & Kourtellos, A. (2010b). Regression models with mixed sampling frequencies. *Journal of Econometrics*, 158(2), 246–261.

Andreou, E., Ghysels, E. & Kourtellos, A. (2013). Should macroeconomic forecasters use daily financial data and how? *Journal of Business and Economic Statistics*, 31(2), 240–251.

Aruoba, S.B., Diebold, F.X. & Scotti, C. (2009). Real-time measurement of business conditions. *Journal of Business and Economic Statistics*, 27(4), 417–427.

Ayllón, A. & Gábos, A. (2017). The interrelationships between the Europe 2020 poverty and social exclusion indicators. *Social Indicators Research*, 130(3), 1025–1049.

Bram, J. & Ludvigson, S. (1998). Does consumer confidence forecast household expenditure? A sentiment index horse race. *Economic Policy Review, Federal Reserve Bank of New York*, 4(2), 59–78.

Čižmešija, M., Sorić, P. & Lolić, I. (2018). The role of economic sentiment in explaining macroeconomic trends, methodological improvements and new areas of application in Croatia, Zagreb. *Faculty of Economics and Business*.

Clements, M.P. & Galvão, A.B. (2009). Forecasting US output growth using leading indicators: An appraisal using MIDAS models. *Journal of Applied Econometrics*, 24(7), 1187–1206.

Clements, M.P. & Galvão, A.B. (2008). Macroeconomic forecasting with mixed-frequency data, Forecasting output growth in the United States. *Journal of Business and Economic Statistics*, 26(4), 546–554.

Corluy, V. & Vandenbroucke, F. (2017). Individual employment, household employment and risk of poverty in the EU. A decomposition analysis. In: A.B. Atkinson and A.-C. Guio I Eric Marlier (eds.), *Monitoring Social Inclusion in Europe, Statistical Books Eurostat*. Luxembourg: Publications Office of the European Union.

Cotsomitis, J.A. & Kwan, A.C.C. (2006). Can consumer confidence forecast household spending? Evidence from the European Commission Business and Consumer Surveys. *Southern Economic Journal*, 72(3), 597–610.

Duarte, C. (2014). Autoregressive augmentation of MIDAS regressions. Working Papers w201401, Banco de Portugal, Economics and Research Department.

ECB (2019). Financial stability review. Retrieved from: https://www.ecb.europa.eu/pub/financial-stability/fsr/html/ecb.fsr201905~266e856634.en.html#toc3 [Accessed on August 30, 2019].

European Commission (2019a). The Joint Harmonised EU Programme of Business and Consumer Surveys, User Guide, European Economy, Directorate-General for Economic and financial affairs.

European Commission (2019b). Consumer, Seasonally Adjusted Data — Database Retrieved from https://ec.europa.eu/info/business-economy-euro/indicators-statistics/economic-databases/business-and-consumer-surveys/download-business-and-consumer-survey-data/time-series_en [Accessed on August 30, 2019].

Eurostat (2006). Comparative EU statistics on income and living conditions, issues and challenges, *Proceedings of the EU-SILC Conference*, Helsinki, November 6–8, 2006, Brussels.

Eurostat (2019). Database. Retrieved from: http://ec.europa.eu/eurostat/data/database [Accessed on August 30, 2019].

Foroni, C., Marcellino, M. & Schumacher, C. (2015). Unrestricted mixed data sampling (MIDAS), MIDAS regressions with unrestricted lag polynomials. *Journal of the Royal Statistical Society, Series A*, 178, 57–82.

Forsberg, L. & Ghysels, E. (2007). Why do absolute returns predict volatility so well? *Journal of Financial Econometrics*, 5(1), 31–67.

Ghysels, E., Sinko, A. & Valkanov, R. (2006b). MIDAS regressions, further results and new directions. *Econometric Reviews*, 26, 53–90.

Ghysels, E. & Valkanov, R. (2012). Forecasting volatility with MIDAS. In: L Bauwens, C. Hafner and S. Laurent (eds.), *Handbook of Volatility Models and Their Applications.* John Wiley & Sons, New Jersey, USA. pp. 383–401.

Ghysels, E., Kvedaras, V. & Zemlys, V. (2016). Mixed frequency data sampling regression models. The R Package MIDASR. R package version 0.6.

Ghysels, E., Santa-Clara, P. & Valkanov, R. (2003). Predicting volatility, getting the most out of return data sampled at different frequencies, Working paper.

Ghysels, E., Kvedaras, V. & Zemlys-Balevičius, V. (2019). Mixed data sampling (MIDAS) regression models. *Handbook of Statistics*, 42, 117–153.

Ghysels, E., Santa-Clara, P. & Valkanov, R. (2005). There is a risk-return tradeoff after all. *Journal of Financial Economics*, 76, 509–548.

Ghysels, E., Santa-Clara, P. & Valkanov, R. (2002). The MIDAS touch, Mixed data sampling regression models, Working paper, UNC and UCLA.

Ghysels, E., Santa-Clara, P. & Valkanov, R. (2006a). Predicting volatility, getting the most out of return data sampled at different frequencies. *Journal of Econometrics*, 131, 59–95.

Ghysels, E., Sinko, S. & Valkanov, R. (2004). The cross-section of firm stock returns and economic announcements. A *Bird's Eye View*, Working paper, UNC and UCSD.

Ghysels, E., Sinko, A., Valkanov, R. (2007). MIDAS regressions: Further results and new directions. *Econometric Views*, 26(1), 53–90. doi: 10.2139/ssrn.885683.

Guagnano, G., Santerelli, E. & Santini, I. (2016). Can social capital affect subjective poverty in Europe? An empirical analysis based on a generalized ordered logit model. *Social Indicators Research*, 128(2), 881–907.

Kelley, C.T. (1999). Iterative methods for optimization. *SIAM Frontiers in Applied Mathematics*, 18, ISBN 0-89871-433-8.

Klein, L.R. & Özmucur, S. (2010). The use of consumer and business surveys in forecasting. *Economic Modeling*, 27(6), 1453–1462.

Krell, K., Frick, J.R. & Grabka, M.M. (2017). Measuring the consistency of cross-sectional and longitudinal income information in EU-SILC. *The Review of Income and Wealth*, 63(1), 30–52.

Kurnoga, N. & Čižmešija, M. (2016). Can consumer survey produce a new measure of household financial distress? *Croatian Operational Research Review*, 7(2), 189–200.

Kvedaras, V. & Zemlys, V. (2012). Testing the functional constraints on parameters in regressions with variables of different frequency. *Economics Letters*, 116(2), 250–254.

Kvedaras, V. & Zemlys, V. (2013). The statistical content and empirical testing of the MIDAS restrictions. Unpublished manuscript.

Lohmann, H. (2011). Comparability of EU-condition survey and register data. The relationship among employment, earnings and poverty. *Journal of European Social Policy*, 21(1), 37–54.

Ludvigson, S. (2004). Consumer confidence and consumer spending. *Journal of Economic Perspectives*, 18, 29–50.

Navicke, J., Rastrigina, O. & Sutherland, H. (2014). Nowcasting indicators of poverty risk in the European Union: A microsimulation approach. *Social Indicators Research*, 119(1), 101–119.

Nikoloski, Z. (2010). Impact of financial crises on poverty in developing world: An empirical approach. Available at SSRN: https://ssrn.com/abstract=1701894.

Rastrigina, O., Leventi, C. & Holly, S. (2015). Nowcasting risk of poverty and low work intensity in Europe, EUROMOD Working paper EM9/15. Retrieved from: https,//www.econstor.eu/handle/10419/113340 [Accessed on August 30, 2019].

Rewilak, J. (2018). The impact of financial crises on the poor. *Journal of International Development*, 30, 1–19.

Strutz, T. (2016). A practical introduction to weighted least squares and beyond. In: *Data Fitting and Uncertainty*, 2nd edition. Springer, Germany.

The Guardian (2019). Global recession a serious danger in 2020, says UN. Retrieved from: https://www.theguardian.com/business/2019/sep/25/global-recession-a-serious-danger-in-2020-says-un.

UN (2015). Transforming our world: the 2030 Agenda for Sustainable Development Resolution 70/1 adopted by the UN General Assembly. Retrieved from: http://www.un.org/ga/search/view_doc.asp?symbol=A/RES/70/1&Lang=E [Accessed on August 30, 2019].

Whelan, C.T., Nolan, B. & Maitre, B. (2014). Multidimensional poverty measurement in Europe. An application of the adjusted headcount approach. *Journal of European Social Policy*, 24(2), 183–197.

Chapter 6

What Drives Regional Innovation Capacity Build-Up in China?

Xiaohua Yang[*,§], Ying Zhou[†], Roger (Rongxin) Chen[*]
and Richard Carney[‡]

[*]University of San Francisco, San Francisco, CA 94117, USA

[†]Nanjing Audit University, Gulou, Nanjing, China

[‡]China Europe International Business School, Pudong, Shanghai, China

[§]yuxiyulu@126.com

Building innovation capacity in China is critical to continuing economic development. This study adopts regional innovation system (RIS) and regional innovation capacity (RIC) approaches to investigate the relatively new phenomenon of RIC and identify key factors that explain variations in innovation capacity across regions of China. Our study empirically shows that the key drivers of RIC differ substantively between radical innovation and incremental innovation. Specifically, our findings suggest that innovation capacity is largely related to innovation inputs and these inputs tend to affect incremental innovation more than radical innovation in the context of China. The second finding is a relatively new phenomenon, which we explain using the continuum of CME-LME. Our study contributes to the literature on RIC in a transitional economic context and provides a number of implications for future studies on RIC. The findings also provide significant implications for government policymakers.

Introduction

Regional innovation is a key driver for the development of emerging economies. Ahlstrom *et al.* (2018) suggested that a solid perception of economic growth in a transition economy requires a good understanding of the regional innovation system (RIS) and regional innovation capacity (RIC). Yet, as it is a relatively new phenomenon, research on the key drivers of RIC remains inadequate. Since the emergence of the framework of national innovation capacity (NIC) in 2000, scholars have made efforts to examine the drivers of NIC and RIC using a quantitative approach (Furman *et al.*, 2002; Hu & Mathews, 2005). Following Furman *et al.*'s (2002) framework, Hu and Mathews (2005) examined the determinants of NIC in East Asia, including concentration on R&D inputs, cluster-specific innovation environment and accumulated knowledge capacity. Such analysis may not, however, be applicable to China's RIC. First, there are inherent differences in the innovation systems between China and other countries. China is the world's second-largest economy, but the development of its innovation systems has fallen behind that of advanced economies. China's RISs were developed unevenly due to the vast differences in economic development across regions in China (Edquist, 2004). Second, their analysis focused on the national level, but the determinants of RIC may be different from those affecting NIC, with large variations in innovation among regions, as well as their trajectory of development over time.

Thus, we believe that studying innovation systems at the regional level is critical in large countries like China. This is because regional economic development in large countries tends to be highly heterogeneous (Edquist, 2004), causing tremendous variation in the factors influencing RIC. Tylecote (2006) argued that there is usually a dual technology system in transitional countries. The upper level system, stated as the national innovation system (NIS), focuses on the role of national institutions and the development of advanced technology, while the lower level system, such as the RIS, emphasizes facilitating the innovation activities of locally embedded industries by providing knowledge infrastructure (Lu & Etzkowitz, 2008).

Our phenomenon-drive study strives to capture, describe and conceptualize an emerging phenomenon so that future research can build on it for further theory and research design (Doh, 2015; Schwarz & Stensaker, 2016). We aim to contribute to the research on RIC in the following ways.

First, through a quantitative study, we provide a better understanding of the impact of specific factors in innovation systems that affect RIC in China. Second, we examine RIC by separating incremental and radical innovation capacity, allowing us to examine how different types of RIC develop, which may help researchers to find a more refined approach to study RIC. Third, our findings provide implications for policymakers, suggesting that regional governments should develop strategies that are aligned with the local environment to increase incremental and radical innovation capacities.

Innovation Systems in China

In recent years, the concept of *Innovation Systems* has inspired research and shaped discourse in both academia and policy (see Raska & Hain, 2019 for a review on this topic). Similarly, interest in understanding Chinese innovation system and innovation capacity is growing as innovation and entrepreneurship have become China's national strategy. The innovation system in China has been developing gradually, following the economic transitional path since the foundation of the People's Republic of China (PRC) in 1949. The development of NIS and RIS has been accelerating in recent years, with interest in research on NIS remaining high (Godin, 2009; Guan & Chen, 2012). Innovation, together with entrepreneurship, is viewed as a key driver for China's economic growth (Wang *et al.*, 2008). In fact, "Mass Entrepreneurship and Innovation by All" (大众创业万众创新) has become a national strategy for economic transition (Ahlstrom *et al.*, 2018).

As shown in Figure 1, however, the regions in China are unevenly developed. This figure clusters regions based on the economic development level measured by GDP per capita, with a few regions high above, and some quite below, the nation average. For instance, Shanghai, Beijing and Tianjin are well above the national average, but Guizhou and Gansu are way below.

Similar to economic development, the innovation development of each region has its own characteristics. For example, capital investment, an important factor in innovation performance (Liu & Zou, 2008), is quite different among regions in China. Figure 2 shows that capital investment in innovation development has been changing in most of the regions, but Beijing remains the most aggressive, spending about 10–15% of its GDP on science and technology (S&T) activities in 2008, followed by

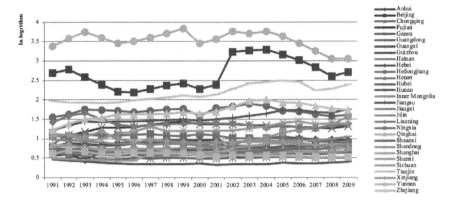

Figure 1.   Ratio of regional GDP per capita to national GDP per capita
Source: CSY 1992 to CSY 2010.

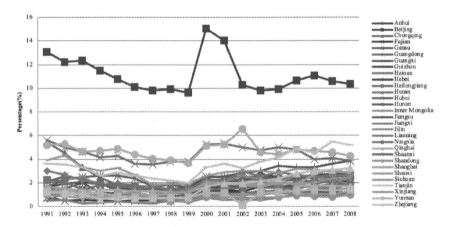

Figure 2.   Regional science and technology funding intensity
Note: S&T Funding Intensity = (S&T Funding/GDP) × 100.
Source: Calculated based on the data collected from CSY and CSYST 1992–2009.

Shanghai, Tianjin and Jiangsu. Most of the regions allocate less than 4% of GDP to S&T activities.

In addition, the innovation performance, measured by patent grants, reveals the variation of RIC in China. Figure 3 shows how the number of patents granted to each region has been growing at different rates and the disparity of innovation capacity between high and low innovative regions

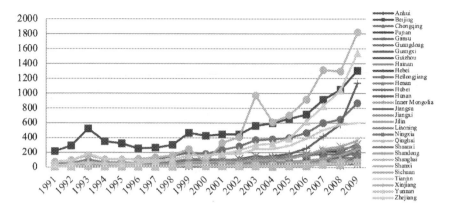

Figure 3. Regional patent grants per million people

Source: Calculated based on the data collected from PSY 1992 to PSY 2010.

is increasing. In 2009, around 60% of patent grants were from the five most innovative regions, Shanghai, Zhejiang, Beijing, Jiangsu and Guangdong. Comparing Figures 2 and 3, we find that the regions that invest the most in S&T activities may not be the most innovative regions based on patent grants. Evidently, the difference in the development of innovation capacity among regions in China is vast.

Conceptual and Empirical Models

Since the emergence of the framework of NIC in 2000, there has been a rush to establish an index system for NIS and RIS (Bao, 2010), as well as to quantitatively examine the drivers of NIC and RIC (Furman *et al.*, 2002; Hervas-Oliver & Dalmau-Porta, 2007). Investigating the differences in innovation capacity among countries, Furman *et al.* (2002) developed the NIC framework, which consists of common innovation infrastructure, cluster-specific environments for innovation, and the quality of linkages between them. Following Furman *et al.* (2002), Hu and Mathews (2005) investigated the determinants of NIC in East Asia. The NIC theoretical framework is not, however, directly applicable to China, as there are inherent differences in the innovation systems between China and more developed countries (Gu & Lundvall, 2006; Liu & White, 2001). Furthermore, these studies focused on NIC, not RIC. To study innovation capacity at the regional level in China, Li (2009) adapted Furman's framework along with the RIS approach.

Conceptual model

The concept of RIS emerged in the early 1990s. Prior studies argued that RIS plays crucial roles in developing RIC. RIS is the infrastructure of RIC, outlining how to set up key drivers in innovation processes (Asheim & Isaksen, 1997; Cooke, Uranga, & Etxebarria, 1997) within a country or a region; thus, RIC depends on the development of RIS. Though there are no commonly accepted definitions of RIS, important components of RIS are innovation actors, institutional environments and interactions among innovation actors both within and outside a region (Asheim & Isaksen, 1997; Sawang, Zhou, & Yang, 2017). The main limitation of the RIS approach is its lack of an overarching logic for how these multiple dimensions fit together to produce innovation outcomes.

We address this shortcoming in the development of our theoretical approach by drawing on related work that also examines the interrelations among innovation actors and the institutional environment, known as the varieties of capitalism (VoC) framework (Hall & Soskice 2001). This framework is often grouped together with the broader business systems literature (Whitley, 2010; Redding, 2005). According to the VoC approach, institutional environments in advanced economies are arrayed along a continuum, with coordinated market economies (CMEs) at one end (e.g. Germany) and liberal market economies (LMEs) at the other (e.g. the United States). In CMEs, coordination among economic actors is encouraged and preserved; in LMEs, economic actors are more transactional.

Collectively, market institutions complement one another, encouraging a focus on either the long term, as in Germany, or the short term, as in the United States. In Germany, firm strategies compatible with these institutional incentives tend to focus on the cultivation of highly specialized niche products that preserve the firm's market competitiveness via incremental innovation. In the United States, by contrast, capital and labor are far more mobile. This is compatible with the creation of companies that exploit new ideas and technologies, including those that might be disruptive.

The institutions emphasized in the RIS framework differ from the VoC framework, but the same logic can be applied. Specifically, we focus on the following three key RIS drivers: innovation actors, innovation inputs and knowledge interactions/flow. Innovation actors generate, use and diffuse innovation by interacting under the specific institutional arrangements within a region (Chung, 2002). Innovation inputs are an important characteristic of the innovation environment or local context of each region, and knowledge interactions/flow are important indicators of local networks or the interactions between innovation actors. We expect that innovation, either of the radical or incremental type, will be more prevalent in more economically developed regions; however, the RIS framework does not yield clear predictions regarding which innovation type will be more likely. Less developed regions will not display a clear orientation toward either innovation type.

Empirical model

The econometric model, which considers both time-variant and time-invariant variables, is well suited to investigate the influence of innovation system components on RIC in the above framework. Following Furman *et al.* (2002) and Li (2009), we used a fixed effect model, which is appropriate because it accounts for unobserved factors that will affect RIC (which is fixed over time) (Allison, 2009). In this study, in addition to the factors that have been considered, we can expect many idiosyncratic regional differences that affect innovation capacity, such as specific industry sectors.

The general form for a fixed effect model is

$$y_{it} = \alpha + \beta x_{it} + \mu_i + \varepsilon_{it} \quad i = 1,2,\ldots,I, \quad t = 1,2,\ldots,T, \tag{1}$$

where i represents the cross-sectional unit and t represents time; y_{it} is the dependent variable; β is the coefficient for the independent variable; X_{it} represents one independent variable; α is the intercept; μ is the unobserved unit effect; and ε_{it} is the error term.

Transforming innovation effort into innovation capacity, as well as processing a patent application, takes time. Li (2009) indicates that an invention patent usually takes about 3 years, and a utility model patent 1 year, to be granted. A study using patents filed at the Chinese State Intellectual Property Office (CSIPO) finds that the average duration of invention patent examination is 4.71 years (Wagner & Liegsalz, 2011). Because of these different opinions and findings, we follow Li's (2009) long-lag scenario, using 4 years as the lag between inputs and grants.

Substituting the measures selected into the generic fixed effect model, we get the following model for this study:

$$RIC_{i(t+4)} = \alpha + \beta_x \, X_{it}^{\text{In-actor}} + \beta_y \, Y_{it}^{\text{In-input}} + \beta_z \, Z_{it}^{\text{interaction}} + \mu_i + \varepsilon_{it}, \qquad (2)$$

where $RIC_{i(t+4)}$ is the innovation capacity of region i in year t, $X_{it}^{(\text{In-actor})}$ refers to the actors who execute innovation activities, $Y_{it}^{(\text{In-input})}$ refers to the financial and human resources that are invested in innovation activities, and $Z_{it}^{\text{interaction}}$ refers to the interactions between innovation actors within and outside the region.

Empirical Test: To estimate the empirical model, we constructed a dataset covering 30 provincial regions in China from 1991 to 2009. There are 33 administrative regions in China, including 22 provinces, four municipalities, five autonomous regions and two special administrative regions. For this study, we focused on 30 out of 33 regions. We excluded Tibet, Macau and Hong Kong due to their uniqueness and major differences with other regions in China.

Data and summaries

All data for this study are from the Patent Statistic Yearbook (PSY) from 1991 to 2009, the China Statistic Yearbook (CSY) from 1992 to 2009, and the China Statistic Yearbook on Science and Technology (CSYST) from 1992 to 2009. The definition and sources of each variable used in this empirical analysis are listed in Table 1.

To enable comparison of regions with vastly different sizes, all money-related variables are divided by regional GDP and other variables are divided by regional population. We take the logarithm of most metric variables to ensure distributions are approximately normal. Employment rate was not normalized as it is approximately normally distributed.

Dependent variables

Patent data are the most commonly used indicators for measuring innovation output. Although patent information is not perfect, it provides a fairly reliable measure of innovation activity (Acs *et al.*, 2002), and patent statistics offer the best available output indicators for innovation activities

Table 1.   Definitions and sources of variables

Variable	Definition	Source
Dependent Variables		
Radical IC	The number of granted invention patents per million people (in logarithm)	PSY: 1995–2009
Incremental IC	The number of granted utility model patents per million people (in logarithm)	
Independent Variables		
Innovation Actors		
HEI	Number of higher education institutions (HEI) per billion people (in logarithm)	CSY: 1992–2006 CSYST: 1992–2006
LME	Number of large and medium-sized industrial enterprises (LME) per million people (in logarithm)	
Innovation Inputs		
GDPpp	GDP per person (in logarithm)	CSY: 1992–2006
FST	Funding for science and technology (FST) activities per thousand GDP (in logarithm)	CSY: 1992–2006 CSYST: 1992–2006
SE	Full time employed scientists and engineers per million person (in logarithm)	
Employment	Employment rate	CSY: 1992–2006
Knowledge Interaction/Flow		
FDI	Inward foreign direct investment per thousand GDP (in logarithm)	CSY: 1992–2006
Inter-Trade	Import and export trade per thousand GDP	
Domestic-interaction	Value of Domestic technology contract per thousand GDP (in logarithm)	CSYST: 1992–2006

(Freeman, 2004). Domestic patents are more suitable than international patents for this study, as international patents do not reflect the entire spectrum of innovative activities, especially in a transitioning country (Krammer, 2009), whereas domestic patents are more comparable at the regional level. For the RIC pertaining to radical and incremental innovations, we use Chinese law to operationalize the variables. According to the Patent Law in China, invention patents are products or methods new to

China and utility model patents are improvements to existing products and methods. This classification fits the definition of radical and incremental innovation developed by Herbig (1994). Radical innovation refers to innovations that serve to create new products and markets (Herbig, 1994), while incremental innovation focuses on modifying and improving an existing product, technology or process (Herbig, 1994). Hence, invention patents can represent radical innovations, while the utility model fits for incremental innovations. Meanwhile, patent grants represent innovations with more commercial value than applications, so we employ both invention patent grants and utility model patent grants to measure radical and incremental innovations, respectively.

Independent variables

- **Innovation actors:** The main innovation actors considered in innovation system are firms, universities and research institutes. In China, universities are referred to as higher education institutions (HEIs), which consist of universities and special colleges (e.g. medical schools, musical colleges and professional technology colleges). Accordingly, the number of HEI per billion people in each region has been included.
- **Large and medium-sized industrial enterprises (LMEs):** There are many types of firms in China that fit the classification criteria, but the number of all types of firms is not accessible for the study period here. Thus, we employed the number of LMEs per million people in each region to explore the influence of firms on RIC.
- **Innovation input:** A range of innovation inputs have been used in previous studies, such as funding for science and technology (S&T) activities, R&D expenditure (Freeman, 2004), scientists and engineers (Lundvall, 2007) and knowledge stock, all of which are considered as the most direct input factors for innovation activities.
- **FST:** With regard to financial input, we include funding for science and technology activities (FST). Since FST can be used for all science and technology-related activities, such as R&D, subsidies for patent applications, purchases or construction of fixed assets, it may better represent the efforts toward innovation development than R&D expenditure does. Previous research shows that funding for patent subsidy programs implemented by each region have played an

important role in the growth of Chinese patenting, which has led to increased innovation capacity (Li, 2012).

- **SE & Employment:** The number of full-time employed scientists and engineers (SE) per million people and employment rate (employment) represent human resources. Scientists and engineers are the most important human resources for innovation development, but they also need support and help with general administrative issues from other staff, which is why employment rate is included.

- **GDPpp:** GDP per capita and patent stock (Furman *et al.*, 2002) are proposed as two indicators for knowledge stock. GDP per capita captures the ability of a country or a region to realize the economic value of its knowledge, while patent stock directly measures the national or regional pool of technology. As GDP per capita is highly correlated with patent grants, and patent grants are used as a dependent variable in the analysis, only GDP per capita is used. Besides, GDP per capita can also represent the economic infrastructure of a region.

- **Knowledge interactions/flow:** Knowledge interactions/flow between innovation actors have been widely recognized to be important activities in the process of innovation development (Cooke & Memedovic, 2003). Through interactions, innovation actors can learn from each other, share knowledge and resources and consequently accelerate the progress of innovation.

- **International interaction:** The development of RIS is becoming more dependent on external linkages (Asheim & Vang, 2006). Regions can access foreign technologies and knowledge through FDI, international trade and mobility of human capital across borders and collaborations (Liang, 2008; Peng & Wang, 2000; Zhang & Rogers, 2009). Domestic innovation actors can benefit from both foreign technology providers and users. Inflow FDI may bring financial capital, human capital and advanced technologies (Madariaga & Poncet, 2007). International trade may bring advanced technologies, whereby foreign users may facilitate exporters to improve their products to meet the criteria of foreign markets (Lin & Lin, 2010). Liu and Chen (2012) suggested that MNCs pursuing home-based technology exploitation strategies in developing host countries tended to locate their subsidies in a host region with a strong knowledge application and exploitation subsystem, which could produce spillover effects for the local country.

Therefore, we use annual inflow of FDI and the sum of export and import (Inter-Trade) to measure international knowledge interactions/flow.

- **Domestic-interaction:** With respect to domestic interactions, Li (2009) used the proportion of science and technology funds raised by universities and research institutes from firms to measure financial interactions. Contract value in the regional technology market was then used to measure interactive learning. In view of knowledge and data accessibility for such a long period, only the value of the domestic technology contract (VDTC) has been included in this chapter. VDTC here represents knowledge flow and interactive learning, both across and within regions.

Analysis of key results

We collected 450 pieces of data for each variable, including 15 years for 30 regions. The standard deviations show that there are big differences of innovation capacity among regions, as well as some of the innovation inputs (e.g. FST and knowledge interaction/flow) (see Table 2).

Table 3 is a correlation table which shows that most independent variables are not highly correlated. This reduces the overall risk of multicollinearity; however, we found that SE is noticeably correlated with HEIs

Table 2. Descriptive statistics of variables

	N	Period T	Mean.	Min.	Max.	Std. Dev
Radical IC	450	1995–2009	0.61	−1.01	2.72	0.65
Incremental IC	450	1995–2009	1.53	0.56	2.84	0.44
HEI	450	1991–2005	2.98	2.35	3.72	0.24
LME	450	1991–2005	1.20	0.56	2.05	0.28
GDPpp	450	1991–2005	3.75	2.94	4.71	0.34
FST	450	1991–2005	1.19	0.05	2.18	0.31
SE	450	1991–2005	3.08	2.35	4.26	0.35
Employment	450	1991–2005	0.52	0.35	0.67	0.06
FDI	450	1991–2005	1.30	−0.44	2.38	0.52
Inter-trade	450	1991–2005	2.20	1.50	3.36	0.43
Domestic-interaction	450	1991–2005	0.56	−1.26	1.85	0.48

Table 3. Correlations of variables

	Radical IC	Incremental IC	HEI	LME	GDPpp	FST	SE	Employment	FDI	Inter-trade	Domestic-interaction
Radical IC	1										
Incremental IC	0.85**	1									
HEI	0.72**	0.66**	1								
LME	0.56**	0.75**	0.56**	1							
GDPpp	0.88**	0.85**	0.65**	0.65**	1						
FST	0.56**	0.57**	0.63**	0.46**	0.31**	1					
SE	0.73**	0.79**	0.80**	0.73**	0.60**	0.85**	1				
Employment	0.18**	0.22**	-0.01	0.22**	0.16**	0.23**	0.18**	1			
FDI	0.32**	0.44**	0.24**	0.54**	0.50**	0.09	0.29**	0.12*	1		
Inter-trade	0.49**	0.68**	0.48**	0.73**	0.60**	0.35**	0.56**	0.06	0.66**	1	
Domestic-interaction	0.50**	0.54**	0.46**	0.48**	0.40**	0.56**	0.61**	0.12**	0.23**	0.40**	1

Notes: **Correlation is significant at the 0.01 level (2-tailed).
*Correlation is significant at the 0.05 level (2-tailed).

and FST. Because these are important independent variables, we are not able to completely remove them from the empirical model. According to Frost (2017), such multicollinearity only "reduces the statistic power of the model", meaning not only that the related independent variables, such as SE, HEI and FST, are less likely show statistically significant effects but also that it will "not influence the predictions, precision of the predictions, and the goodness-of-fit statistics" (Frost, 2017).

In the following, the estimated results of the empirical framework are explained, and the reasons for the disparity among the influences on different innovations are explored. Table 4 shows the estimated results and depicts that there are disparities between radical and incremental innovations of each exploratory variable.

Table 4.   Estimated results on drivers of RIC in China

		Radical IC	Incremental IC
Innovation actors	HEI	−0.41	0.26***
		(0.39)	(0.09)
	LME	−0.74**	0.05
		(0.32)	(0.07)
Innovation input	GDPpp	5.38***	0.81***
		(0.19)	(0.04)
	FST	1.45***	0.12*
		(0.28)	(0.06)
	SE	1.32***	0.29***
		(0.41)	(0.09)
	Employment	−1.00	0.24
		(1.05)	(0.24)
Knowledge interaction/flow	FDI	−0.58***	−0.16***
		(0.11)	(0.02)
	Inter-Trade	−0.45**	0.42***
		(0.22)	(0.05)
	Domestic Interaction	0.24**	−0.03
		(0.11)	(0.02)
	_cons	−19.83***	−3.86***
		(.097)	(0.22)
	Within R^2	0.88	0.84

Note: Standard errors are in parentheses, ***$p < 0.01$, **$p < 0.05$, *$p < 0.1$.

Innovation actors

Innovation actors contribute to the development of RIC, but they contribute differently to radical and incremental innovation capacity.

HEI: As an innovation actor, HEIs only show significant positive impacts on regional incremental innovation capacity ($b = 0.258$; $p < 0.01$). This implies that the research networks of HEIs in China are successful in helping incremental innovation, but HEIs do not seem to affect radical innovation.

The different impacts of HEI on radical and incremental innovation capacity may be explained by how R&D funding is distributed among different types of research (Zhou *et al.*, 2016). During the period between 1997 and 2005, less than 25% of R&D funding was spent on basic research, more than 50% on applied research and the rest allocated to experimental development in HEI in China (detailed information can be found from CSYST 1998 to CSYST 2006). As basic research mainly leads to radical innovations, and applied research mainly results in incremental innovations, it is not surprising that HEI has a stronger impact on incremental, rather than radical, innovation capacity given the funding allocation structure.

LME showed a negative impact on the radical innovation capacity of regions ($b = -0.744$, $p < 0.05$), while no such negative effect is observed between LME and incremental innovation. This suggests that many LMEs are less likely to place their resources toward radical innovations and are more likely to engage in incremental innovation activities, as incremental innovations are more easily granted (Sun & Du, 2010). This is consistent with a prior study that determined that Chinese companies rely on their overseas subsidiaries to transfer capabilities to parent companies in China (Peng *et al.*, 2017) instead of engaging in radical innovation.

In this regard, ownership may matter. Our further analysis showed that during the research period 1992–2005, foreign-invested enterprises (FIEs) and state-owned enterprises (SOEs) accounted for more than 50% of LME, though the structure of LME had been changing from 1998 to 2005 with the privatization of SOEs. SOEs have lagged in technology development and may be less motivated to acquire new knowledge and to innovate than private enterprises, whether because of government control, subsidies and/or other forms of assistance, as well as pressure for social responsibility, including expansion of employment (Li *et al.*, 2001).

These adversary conditions cause SOEs to be less willing to embark on risky radical innovations. For FIEs, radical innovations may especially serve as negative factors to RIC, as they are reluctant to bring technologies to, or file patents in, China due to intellectual property protection concerns (Zhou, 2006).

Innovation input factors

The results for the input factors indicate that, except for employment rate, all other innovation input factors had a positive and significant impact on both incremental and radical innovations. The insignificant impact of employment rate may be a result of the labor intensity of the Chinese economy during the specific research period (1992–2006), given that more employment does not necessarily lead to more innovation. Another factor worth highlighting is that the magnitude of the GDPpp co-efficient for radical innovation far exceeds the co-efficient of all other innovation input variables. Since radical innovations tend to be risker and may require more investment, this result suggests that a significant driver for such risky and radical innovation is the level of economic development, implying that the more affluent regions tend to be more radical innovators. Our findings confirm that innovation capacity is largely related to innovation inputs and that human capital and financial investment efforts are positively related to RIC.

Knowledge interactions/flow factors

The impact of knowledge interactions/flow factors presents a more complicated picture. International interactions mostly exert negative influences, with the exception of international trade on incremental innovation capacity, while domestic interactions only improve radical innovation capacity.

- **FDI:** Our results show a negative effect of FDI on both radical and incremental regional innovation capability; however, the influence is greater on radical innovation than it is on incremental innovation capability. This result offers additional insight on the impact of FDI on China's innovation capacity. There are more studies showing positive effects of FDI on China's innovation (e.g. Ahlstrom *et al.*, 2018; Buckley *et al.*, 2002; Chuang & Hsu, 2004) than those showing negative effects (e.g. Hu & Jefferson, 2002; Hu *et al.*, 2005). Furthermore, many scholars argue that positive effects indicate that FDI brings in spillover benefits to improve China's innovation capacity. The positive spillovers, however, need necessary conditions (Fu, 2008), such as the absorptive capacity of domestic innovators (Cohen & Levinthal, 1989) and the intensity of interactions between foreign and domestic economic actors (Balasubramanyam *et al.*, 1996).

- **Our study highlights the following scenarios:** FIEs may reduce domestic organizations' capabilities of making innovations by providing competitive payoffs to attract outstanding talent from the labor pool (Asheim & Vang, 2006; Huang, 2004; Sun, 2010), thus reducing the accessibility of scientists, engineers and other skilled technicians to domestic organizations (Liu & Zou, 2008), thereby lowering their innovation capacity. FIEs may also redirect innovative activities, such as R&D, back to the parent company in their home country, consequently reducing innovative activities in the host country. FIEs are known to protect their intellectual property and may choose to avoid unnecessary knowledge sharing with domestic firms, universities and research institutes (Fu & Gong, 2011; Zhou, 2006), only investing in employee training when in need of specific capabilities (Asheim & Vang, 2006), thus weakening the effect of learning from FIEs and spillovers from labor turnover.

- **Inter-trade:** Our findings show that international trade (import/export) showed negative effects on radical innovation capacity ($b = -0.435$, $p < 0.05$), but positive impacts on incremental innovation capacity ($b = 0.423$, $p < 0.01$). Both the negative (Sun *et al.*, 2009) and positive effects (Wang & Kafouros, 2009) of international trade on improving innovation capacity have been found in previous studies. On the export side, the positive effect mainly results in spillovers of exports coming from the information gathered from the export market and by competing with foreign firms. Exporters help domestic companies to access diverse knowledge and information in foreign markets, which stimulates Chinese exporters' innovative activities, helping them improve their own products and related incremental innovations (Salomon & Shaver, 2005; Zhang & Rogers, 2009).

    Imports can help domestic organizations take advantage of advanced foreign technologies and knowledge embedded in imported goods, which will allow domestic organizations to upgrade the average technology of the host country through incremental improvement (Chuang & Hsu, 2004; Fu & Gong, 2011). As such, imports can help build absorptive capacity and enhance innovation performance (Cheung, 2010; Cheung & Lin, 2004). The negative effect might come from either exports or imports. Lin and Lin (2010) found that exports did not help product innovation. In addition, Sun (2010) found that importing may be a substitute for radical innovation capacity in domestic organizations. These domestic organizations may be incapable of assimilating and fully utilizing the technologies, knowledge and information embedded in the imports (Yang *et al.*, 2014).

- **Domestic-interaction:** Measured as technology contract value per thousand GDP, domestic interaction significantly improves radical innovation, but has no effect on incremental innovation capacity. This positive and significant effect aligns with the theory that domestic technology transfer helps to generate innovations (Edquist, 1997). Researchers also argue that technology transfer increases patenting in the long run (Sun *et al.*, 2009). The significant impact of domestic interaction also indicates that the technology market plays a critical role in improving China's RIC.

Discussion and Conclusion

Our phenomenon-drive research approach allows us to capture and document the RIC during the period 1991–2005, when China experienced rapid economic growth and ascended into the WTO. This was also the time when the Chinese government designated innovation as its next major growth engine (Schwatz & Stensaker, 2016). As such, our study has a number of significant, tentative findings. First, we are able to verify that RIC is largely related to innovation inputs, including the number of HEIs, the number of large and medium-sized enterprises and the number of scientists and engineers in a region, as well as GDP and FDI and international trade, among others. Second, we empirically demonstrate that the key drivers of RIC differ substantively between radical innovation and incremental innovation. Specifically, our findings suggest that innovation inputs tend to affect incremental innovation, more than radical innovation, in the context of China. Although our findings show the "innovation inputs" positively impact both radical and incremental innovation, these "innovation actors" clearly impact incremental innovation more than radical innovation. This raises the question of what motivates these actors to pursue incremental innovation within the Chinese institutional ecosystem.

The comparison between coordinated and liberal market economies, as manifested by Germany and the United States, can offer helpful insights. When comparing China's market institutions to those of Germany and the United States, we observe they are far more similar to those found in Germany. By placing China along the CME–LME continuum with respect to each of the five market institutions mentioned earlier, we can observe that China has more: (a) concentrated ownership; (b) stable employment; (c) banking-oriented financial systems; (d) vocational training; and (e) firms that are more likely to collaborate with each other than American firms. Notwithstanding, the important regional variation in such a large country as China, we can draw the general conclusion that Chinese firm strategies focusing on incremental innovation are likely to experience better performance over time, since they are compatible with the innovation incentives of the institutional ecosystem in which they are located. Thus, the most effective types of innovation policies are those that complement this pre-existing institutional ecosystem and leverage it to promote incremental forms of innovation. An excellent example of such a policy is the creation of the Fraunhofer Institute in Germany, the largest applied research organization in Europe.

The significant negative impact of FDI on innovation capacity further suggests that increasing FDI alone will not improve the innovation capacity of a region. Policymakers should consider developing infrastructure to enable Chinese firms and institutions to reap the benefits of positive technology spillovers from foreign companies, as simply attracting FDI alone will not lead to those benefits. As a result, the government needs to devise proper policies to create an ecosystem to effectively utilize FDI for the purposes of RIC development. This study does indeed have a few weaknesses. For example, although we find that the impact of international trade on RIC differs between radical and incremental innovation capacity, our data did not allow us to separate exports and imports in this study. To facilitate innovation development through international trade, future studies may separately examine the impact of imports and exports to see if they have different effects on RIC in order to better assist policymakers in making more informed policy decisions. Additionally, our study does not include control variables, upon which future studies may improve.

Another limitation is that this study has yet to identify the levels and differences in the actor groups in the RIS to determine the influences of such actor groups on the development of RIC (Njøs & Fosse, 2019). Our study uses patents counts to measure RIC, which has been questioned in the literature. Future research could use both patent quantity and quality to improve the measurement of innovation and more accurately evaluate the effect of various actors on RIC (Ejermo, 2009). Furthermore, although this study is phenomenon driven, the given data from 1991 to 2005 may not reveal some of the nuances related to the changes and emerging issues from the past 10–15 years in the global economy. Thus, what we captured and described in this study is only applicable to the context of the study, meaning that future research needs to incorporate data collected from 2005 onward to address the above weaknesses. Finally, as indicated earlier, our data show multicollinearity among some independent variables, such as SE, HEI and FST. This typically leads to insignificant results among the independent variables (Frost, 2017). Though our empirical results exhibited many significant impacts predicted by our conceptual model, the potential multicollinearity problem may indeed prevent us from observing some important effects analyzed in our model. This is a weakness that future research should try to avoid.

We suggest that future research should investigate the differences among the actors in the RIS and the mechanisms that such differences lead to in the differences within the RIC. For instance, competition from informal firms (counterfeiting firms) has been found to perhaps trigger more innovation than in formal firms in their region as a result of other factors, such as adoption of a global supply chain system (Heredia Pérez *et al.*, 2019). Future research could also branch out to study innovation capacity at the municipality level, as prior studies have shown that interaction between FDI spatial spillovers and the intensity of industrial agglomeration may have a different impact on municipal innovation capacity within and across cities (Ning *et al.*, 2016). Finally, we encourage more phenomenon-driven research on RIC, as it is an emerging phenomenon that requires capturing, describing, documenting and conceptualizing a reality in a given context, so that we can properly theorize and develop a research design to answer these research questions.

References

Allison, P.D. (2009). *Fixed Effects Regression Models*. Thousand Oaks, California: SAGE.

Acs, Z.J., Anselin, L. & Varga, A. (2002). Patents and innovation counts as measures of regional production of new knowledge. *Research Policy*, 31(7), 1069–1085.

Ahlstrom, D., Yang, X., Wang, L. & Wu, C. (2018). A global perspective of entrepreneurship and innovation in China. *Multinational Business Review*, 26(4), 302–318.

Asheim, B.T. & Isaksen, A. (1997). Location, agglomeration and innovation: Towards regional innovation systems in Norway? *European Planning Studies*, 5(3), 299–330.

Asheim, B.T. & Vang, J. (2006). Regional innovation systems in Asian countries: A new way of exploiting the benefits of transnational corporations. *Innovation: Management, Policy & Practice*, 8(1–2), 27–44.

Balasubramanyam, V.N., Salisu, M. & Sapsford, D. (1996). Foreign direct investment and growth in EP and is countries. *The Economic Journal*, 106(434), 92–105.

Bao, Z. (2010). Construction of industrial technology innovation capability evaluation index system. *International Journal of Business and Management*, 5(12), 220–224.

Buckley, P.J., Clegg, J. & Wang, C. (2002). The impact of inward FDI on the performance of Chinese manufacturing firms. *Journal of International Business Studies*, 33(4), 637–655.

Chen, K. & Guan, J. (2011). Mapping the functionality of China's regional innovation systems: A structural approach. *China Economic Review*, 22(1), 11–27.

Cheung, K.Y. (2010). Spillover effects of FDI via exports on innovation performance of China's high-technology industries. *Journal of Contemporary China*, 19(65), 541–557.

Cheung, K.Y. & Lin, P. (2004). Spillover effects of FDI on innovation in China: Evidence from the provincial data. *China Economic Review*, 15(1), 25–44.

Chuang, Y.C. & Hsu, P.F. (2004). FDI, trade, and spillover efficiency: evidence from China's manufacturing sector. *Applied Economics*, 36(10), 1103–1115.

Chung, S. (2002). Building a national innovation system through regional innovation systems. *Technovation*, 22(8), 485–491.

Cohen, W.M. & Levinthal, D.A. (1989). Innovation and learning: The two faces of R&D. *The Economic Journal*, 99(397), 569–596.

Cooke, P. & Memedovic, O. (2003). *Strategies for Regional Innovation Systems: Learning Transfer and Application*. Vienna: UNIDO.

Cooke, P., Uranga, M.G. & Etxebarria, G. (1997). Regional innovative systems: Institutional and organisational dimensions. *Research Policy*, 26(4,5), 475–491.

Doh, J.P. (2015). From the Editor: Why we need phenomenon-based research in international business. *Journal of World Business*, 4(50), 609–611.

Edquist, C. (1997). *Systems of Innovation: Technologies, Institutions and Organizations*. London: Pinter.

Edquist, C. (2004). Systems of innovation: Perspectives and challenges. In J. Fagerberg, D.C. Mowery, and R.R. Nelson (eds.), *Oxford Handbook of Innovation and Policy*. Oxford: Oxford University Press.

Ejermo, O. (2009). Regional innovation measured by patent data — Does quality matter? *Industry and Innovation*, 16(2), 141–165.

Freeman, C. (2004). Technological infrastructure and international competitiveness. *Industrial and Corporate Change*, 13(3), 541–569.

Frost, J. (2017). Multicollinearity in regression analysis: Problems, detection, and solutions. Retrieved from: https://statisticsbyjim.com/regression/multicollinearity-in-regression-analysis/.

Fu, X. (2008). Foreign direct investment, absorptive capacity and regional innovation capabilities: Evidence from China. *Oxford Development Studies*, 36(1), 89–110.

Fu, X. & Gong, Y. (2011). Indigenous and foreign innovation efforts and drivers of technological upgrading: Evidence from China. *World Development*, 39(7), 1213–1225.

Furman, J.L., Porter, M.E. & Scott, S. (2002). The determinants of national innovative capacity. *Research Policy*, 31(6), 899–933.

Godin, B. (2009). National innovation system: The system approach in historical perspective. *Science, Technology & Human Values*, 34(4), 476–501.

Gu, S. & Lundvall, B.-Å. (2006). China's innovation system and the move towards harmonious growth and endogenous innovation. In: S. Gu (ed.), *Innovation In China: Harmonious Transformation*. Maleny: eContent Management Pty Ltd.

Guan, J. & Chen, K. (2012). Modeling the relative efficiency of national innovation systems. *Research Policy*, 41(1), 102–115.

Hall, P.A. & Soskice, D. (2001). An introduction to varieties of capitalism. In: P.A. Hall and D. Soskice (eds.), *Varieties of Capitalism: The Institutional Foundations of Comparative Advantage*. New York: Oxford University Press, pp. 21–27.

Herbig, P.A. (1994). *The Innovation Matrix: Culture and Structure Prerequisites to Innovation*. Westport, CT: Quorum Books.

Heredia Pérez, J.A., Yang, X., Bai & O, Flores (2019). How does competition from informal firms affect the innovation of formal firms? *International Studies of Management & Organization*, 49 (2), 1–18.

Hervas-Oliver, J.-L. & Dalmau-Porta, J.I. (2007). Which IC components explain national IC stocks? *Journal of Intellectual Capital*, 8(3), 444–469.

Hong, W. (2008). Decline of the center: The decentralizing process of knowledge transfer of Chinese universities from 1985 to 2004. *Research Policy*, 37(4), 580–595.

Hu, A.G. & Jefferson, G.H. (2002). FDI Impact and Spillover: Evidence from China's electronic and textile industries. *World Economy*, 25(8), 1063–1076.

Hu, A.G., Jefferson, G.H. & Qian, J. (2005). R&D and technology transfer: Firm-level evidence from Chinese industry. *The Review of Economics and Statistics*, 87(4), 780–786.

Hu, M.-C. & Mathews, J.A. (2005). National innovative capacity in East Asia. *Research Policy*, 34(9), 1322–1349.

Huang, J.-T. (2004). Spillovers from Taiwan, Hong Kong, and Macau investment and from other foreign investment in Chinese industries. *Contemporary Economic Policy*, 22(1), 13–25.

Krammer, S. (2009). Drivers of national innovation in transition: Evidence from a panel of Eastern European countries. *Research Policy*, 38(5), 845–860.

Li, X. (2009). China's regional innovation capacity in transition: An empirical approach. *Research Policy*, 38(2), 338–357.

Li, X., Liu, X. & Parker, D. (2001). Foreign direct investment and productivity spillovers in the Chinese manufacturing sector. *Economic Systems*, 25(4), 305–321.

Li, X. (2012). Behind the recent surge of Chinese patenting: An institutional view. *Research Policy*, 41(1), 236–249.

Liang, Y. (2008). Why are China's exports special? The role of FDI, regional trade and government policies. *Chinese Economy*, 41(6), 99–118.

Lin, H.-L. & Lin, E.S. (2010). FDI, trade, and product innovation: Theory and evidence. *Southern Economic Journal*, 77(2), 434–464.

Liu, M.C. & Chen, S.H. (2012). MNCs' offshore R&D networks in host country's regional innovation system: The case of Taiwan-based firms in China. *Research Policy*, 41(6), 1107–1120.

Liu, X. & White, S. (2001). Comparing innovation systems: A framework and application to China's transitional context. *Research Policy*, 30(7), 1091–1114.

Liu, X. & Zou, H. (2008). The impact of greenfield FDI and mergers and acquisitions on innovation in Chinese high-tech industries. *Journal of World Business*, 43(3), 352–364.

Lu, L. & Etzkowitz, H. (2008). Strategic challenges for creating knowledge-based innovation in China. *Journal of Technology Management in China*, 3(1), 5–11.

Lundvall, B.-Å. (2007). National innovation systems-analytical concept and development tool. *Industry and Innovation*, 14(1), 95–119.

Madariaga, N. & Poncet, S. (2007). FDI in Chinese cities: Spillovers and impact on growth. *World Economy*, 30(5), 837–862.

Ning, L., Wang, F. & Li, J. (2016). Urban innovation, regional externalities of foreign direct investment and industrial agglomeration: Evidence from Chinese cities. *Research Policy*, 45(4), 830–843.

Njøs, R. & Fosse, J.K. (2019). Linking the bottom-up and top-down evolution of regional innovation systems to policy: organizations, support structures and learning processes. *Industry and Innovation*, 26(4), 419–438.

Peng, M.W. & Wang, D.Y. (2000). Innovation capability and foreign direct investment: Toward a learning option perspective. *Management International Review*, 40, 79–93.

Peng, Z., Qing, C., Chen, R.R., Cannice, M.V. & Yang, X. (2017). Towards a framework of reverse knowledge transfer by emerging economy multinationals: Evidence from Chinese MNE subsidiaries in the United States. *Thunderbird International Business Review*, 59(3), 349–366.

Rakas, M. & Hain, D.S. (2019). The state of innovation system research: what happens beneath the surface? *Research Policy*, 48(9), 103787.

Redding, G. (2005). The thick description and comparison of societal systems of capitalism. *Journal of International Business Studies*, 36(2), 123–155.

Salomon, R.M. & Shaver, J.M. (2005). Learning by exporting: new insights from examining firm innovation. *Journal of Economics & Management Strategy*, 14(2), 431–460.

Sawang, S., Zhou, Y. & Yang, X. (2017). Does institutional context matter in building innovation capability? *International Journal of Technological Learning, Innovation and Development*, 9(2), 153–168.

Sun, W., Peng, J., Ma, J. & Zhong, W. (2009). Evolution and performance of Chinese technology policy: An empirical study based on "market in exchange for technology" strategy. *Journal of Technology Management in China*, 4(3), 195–216.

Sun, Y. (2010). What matters for industrial innovation in China: R&D, technology transfer or spillover impacts from foreign investment? *International Journal of Business and Systems Research (IBSR)*, 4(5–6), 621–647.

Sun, Y. & Du, D. (2010). Determinants of industrial innovation in China: Evidence from its recent economic census. *Technovation*, 30(9–10), 540–550.

Schwarz, G.M. & Stensaker, I.G. (2016). Showcasing phenomenon-driven research on organizational change. *Journal of Change Management*, 16(4), 245–264.

Tylecote, A. (2006). Twin innovation systems, intermediate technology and economic development: history and prospect for China. *Innovation: Management, Policy, & Practice*, 8(1–2), 62.

Wang, C. & Kafouros, M.I. (2009). What factors determine innovation performance in emerging economies? Evidence from China. *International Business Review*, 18(6), 606–616.

Wagner, S. & Liegsalz, J. (2011). Patent examination at the State Intellectual Property office in China. Paper presented at the *Academy of Managment Annual Meeting*, San Antonio, Texas, USA.

Whitley, R. (2010). The institutional construction of firms, In: G. Morgan, J.L. Campbell, C. Crouch, O.K. Pedersen, and R. Whitley (eds.), *The Oxford Handbook of Comparative Institutional Analysis*. Oxford: Oxford University Press, pp. 422–453.

Wooldridge, J.M. (2002). *Econometric Analysis of Cross Section and Panel Data.* Massachusetts: The MIT Press.

Yang, Y., Yang, X., Chen, R.R. & Allen, J.P. (2014). What drives emerging-economy outbound FDI decisions to obtain strategic assets? *Asian Business & Management*, 13(5), 379–410.

Zhang, J. & Rogers, J.D. (2009). The technological innovation performance of Chinese firms: the role of industrial and academic R&D, FDI and the markets in firm patenting. *International Journal of Technology Management*, 48(4), 518–543.

Zhou, Y. (2006). Features and impacts of internationalization of transnational corporations' R&D: China's Case. In: *Globalization of R&D and Developing Countries*. New York and Geneva: UNCTAD, pp. 109–115.

Zhou, Y., Sawang, S. & Yang, X. (2016). Understanding the regional innovation capacity in China after economic reforms. *International Journal of Innovation Management*, 20(06), 1650057.

Chapter 7

Emerging Economies and Talent Management: Core Challenges Facing Key Actors in Strategy Translation

Maria Teresa Beamond[*,§], Elaine Farndale[†]
and Charmine Hartel[‡]

[*]*RMIT University, Melbourne VIC 3000, Australia*

[†]*Pennsylvania State University, PA 16801, USA*

[‡]*Monash University, Clayton VIC 3800, Australia*

[§]*maria.beamond@rmit.edu.au*

An important component of globalization over the past two decades has been emerging economies' rapid integration into the world economy. Consequently, multinational enterprises (MNEs) have faced substantial talent management challenges to attract and retain high-performing employees. We address here the question of how MNEs have tackled these challenges by focusing on Latin America as an example of a region undergoing rapid economic development during the mining industry boom. Based on a case study of one MNE, interview data were collected in Peru, Chile and Argentina at a time of substantial skill shortages in the region. By analyzing the organizational structure of the MNE and its translation of talent management strategies from corporate to subsidiary levels, we explain who the key actors are in the process of translation and identify five key talent management challenges that foreign-owned MNEs face when operating in Latin America.

Introduction

Globalization is contributing to increasing competition for talent among multinational enterprises (MNEs) (Latukha, 2016). Emerging economies are contributing to this "war for talent" as they achieve high-income status (IMF, 2017, p. XIII), and it is estimated that by 2050, the gross domestic product of BRICS (Brazil, Russia, India, China and South Africa) will surpass that of the G7 (the seven largest global economies). Talent management is thus high on MNE agendas, focusing on how to develop efficient human resource management (HRM) activities to attract, identify, develop and retain talented individuals in organizations (Meyers & Van Woerkom, 2014). MNEs adopt talent management strategies to differentiate themselves from their competitors to achieve sustained competitive advantage (Wright *et al.*, 1994). For these strategies to be successful, MNEs need to translate them from the corporate headquarters to the subsidiaries operating in different parts of the world — a task that is challenging at best and disastrous at worst (Beamond *et al.*, 2016). We present here a case study that addresses the following question: what are the core talent management challenges facing key strategic actors in MNEs when operating in emerging economies? Specifically, we describe the situation faced by a large Australian MNE with substantial operations in Latin America, hereafter "ABC" mining (a pseudonym to protect confidentiality). Following a brief overview of the talent management and translation literatures, we describe the organizational structure of our case MNE. We identify who the key actors are in the process of translation of the talent management strategies and explore the key talent management challenges that they are facing. In so doing, we address the lack of empirical research on the Latin American region (Bonache *et al.*, 2012), given the predominance of India and China as the focus of studies in this field to date (e.g. Illes *et al.*, 2010; Tymon *et al.*, 2010).

Talent Management Translation

Although talent represents a source of sustained competitive advantage, scholars and practitioners concur that managing talent is a substantial challenge for MNEs (Meyers & Van Woerkom, 2014), especially in emerging economies due to the unique and little-understood cultural and institutional contexts they represent (Li & Scullion, 2010; Tarique & Schuler, 2010). MNEs from developed economies operating in emerging economy contexts are faced with weak institutional infrastructures generated by economic and political uncertainties and a talent pool that lacks market-based skills (Wright *et al.*, 2005). MNEs thus experience skill shortages to manage in these culturally complex and geographically distant countries, as well as having a shortage of home-grown talent in both their home countries and emerging economies to address this challenge (Latukha, 2016). In addition to talent shortages, MNEs face the complex task of translating their corporate talent management strategies to subsidiaries in emerging economies (Beamond *et al.*, 2019). We use the translation concept used in this chapter to describe how the constant flow of management ideas and practices are resulting in new ideas, when they from their origins to other places; these new ideas are then created through both transference and transformation (Czarniawska & Sevon, 2005). In the remainder of this chapter, we present the case of ABC, an Australian MNE operating in Latin America, describing the key actors and their challenges in translating talent management strategy across the firm's operations.

Methodology

A case study design allows the researcher to address "how" and "why" questions when they have little control over events (Yin, 2017). This method facilitates an in-depth understanding of talent management strategy translation, building on data collected during a time of substantial skill shortages in the Latin American region due to the boom in the global mineral resources mining industry. Data were collected from the case MNE through qualitative standardized open-ended interviews (Patton, 1990). Participants from the MNE were selected in conjunction with the vice president of HRM and the first author based on the availability of staff and incorporating respondents from different organizational levels and locations. Interviews were recorded, transcribed and translated into English. The analysis of the data was conducted by following stepwise thematic analysis (Braun & Clarke, 2006). Hence, interview transcripts were first read and re-read several times to become familiar with the data, from which the key themes emerged. Evidence from the in-depth interviews was used to elucidate the ideas identified from the talent management and translation literatures (Graebner *et al.*, 2012), to verify the theoretical relationships, and hence to identify core talent management translation actors and challenges. In total, interview data were gathered

Table 1. Number of interviews and mining site operations

Country	Operation	Commute	Estimated travel time each way	Interviewees
Peru	Rural mine	Fly-in/Fly-out	10 hours from Lima (Flight and 8 hours by road)	12
	Rural mine	Fly-in/Fly-out	8 hours from Lima (Flight and 7 hours by road)	18
Chile	Rural mine	Daily commute	2 hours from Antofagasta: 4 hours per day	17
	Rural copper smelter	Daily commute	1 hour from Antofagasta: 2 hours per day	15
Argentina	Rural mine	Fly-in/Fly-out	8 hours (Flight and road)	17
Chile/Peru	Urban HQ	N/A	N/A	13

from 92 respondents over a nine-week period from offices of the head-quarters (HQ), five mines and one copper smelter in Peru, Chile and Argentina in late 2011 (see Table 1).

Sixteen interviewees were women of whom 50% held superintendent positions, 45% had other positions below supervisors and 5% were supervisors. Most interviewees had been working in the company for 1–5 years, although this varied by location due to when a mine had been constructed. Some of the older mines had experienced different ownership and acquisitions, consequently having witnessed different types of practices. People who had a long tenure at a mine possessed valuable, inimitable and difficult-to-replicate tacit knowledge. This knowledge was not only within the technical and managerial areas where people had worked but also in the intrinsic work environment that each mining operation had developed after experiencing different acquisitions. Moreover, these long-serving employees had achieved internal and external legitimacy in the eyes of people working inside the mining operation and from the community, other stakeholders and contractors. Table 2 summarizes other interviewee characteristics.

ABC's Translation of Talent Management to Subsidiaries

Organization structure

ABC mining had invested more than six billion dollars in its operations in Latin America, and at the time of this study, executives were very

Table 2.   Characteristics of interviewees

Characteristics	Categories	Number of interviewees
Gender	Female	16
	Male	76
Hierarchical position	CEO	1
	Executives	7
	Managers	19
	Superintendents/Supervisors	53
	Other	12
Time working in the company	Less than 1 year	8
	1–5 years	34
	5–10 years	15
	10–15 years	25
	15–25 years or more	10
Education Level	Undergraduate	44
	Postgraduate (Masters)	45
	Research (PhD)	2
	Other	1
Age (years)	25–35	20
	35–45	29
	45–55	35
	55–65	8

concerned about their ability to attract necessary talent in key positions in its subsidiaries. To understand the importance of talent within ABC, we start with a description of the organizational structure, as Figure 1 shows. ABC mining's operations totaled about 70,000 employees and contractors worldwide at the time of the data collection (late 2011). Figure 1 depicts the organizational structure of ABC and its subsidiaries in Peru, Chile and Argentina. ABC has five levels: corporate headquarters (HQH), business unit headquarters (HQ) and subsidiaries that include regional head offices (RHs), host-country head offices (HC) and regional or provincial businesses (RB).

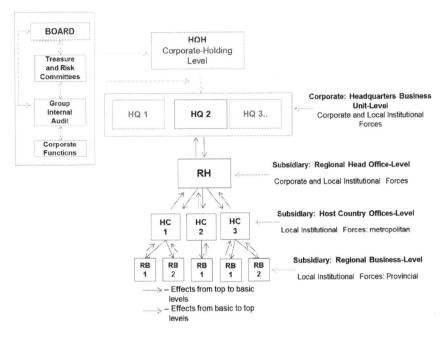

Example of a Business Unit and its Subsidiary in the
Emerging Markets of Latin America

Figure 1.   ABC's organizational structure with subsidiaries in Latin America

In 2011, ABC was listed on the London and Swiss stock exchanges and was structured by commodity lines or business units, each operating as a global business. ABC maintained a corporate center of about 50 staff to avoid duplication with the commodity line and was located in two head offices in Switzerland and the UK (level 1, HQH corporate holding in Figure 1). The corporation's core business approach, known as *sustainable development policy and standards*, was developed by the decision-makers from the corporate board. This study focuses on one of ABC's commodity business units, depicted in Figure 1 as HQ business unit 2 or HQ 2. Headquartered in Australia, HQ 2 was created in 2004 and had a decentralized management structure. The principles of this business unit were based on the corporate *sustainable development policy*. By 2010, the business unit had doubled its annual mined commodity production substantially in the world producer rankings. Pressures such as shareholder requirements, the global focus of the management team and key talent demands internationally were driving the company to seek superior performance. With an average of 30,000 employees in 2011, HQ 2 was operating in eight countries — Australia, Argentina, Chile, Peru, Canada, USA, Philippines and Papua New Guinea — of which five were in emerging economies. We focus here on the operations in the emerging economies of Latin America (Peru, Chile and Argentina) where HQ 2 had significant investments. According to reports from the HR department at HQ, ABC would need some 14,000 employees to develop its projects over the coming 4 years. The Latin America regional head office (see Figure 1: level 3, RH) was dually located in both Chile and Australia, meaning the CEO was travelling regularly between the two countries. HQ 2 received instructions from decision-makers at HQH to translate and implement corporate talent management strategies to all levels of the organization. Although HQ 2 was located in Chile, the VP of Operations for Latin America was located in Peru due to important investments there. The regional head offices (RH) represent HQ 2's subsidiaries and embody two contexts: the host-country office (HC) and the regional businesses (RB). The RHs are commonly situated in the major cities (i.e. Lima, Santiago and Buenos Aires) while regional businesses or mining operations are located in rural areas. Each level (HQ 2, RH, HC and RB) has its own organizational structure. A typical RB organizational hierarchy includes general managers, managers, superintendents, supervisors, professionals and operators. Most rural mining operations are in the Andes Mountains, between 2,000 and 5,000 m above sea-level and between 3 and 8 h drive to the closest town. Therefore, most of the staff there are *employed* on a *fly-in fly-out basis. The case demonstrates the complexities of translating corporate strategies when the organizational structure incorporates operations in both developed and emerging economies, located in urban and rural locations, with different groups of employees with distinct cultural backgrounds, and all exposed to different institutional environments.*

Key actors in translation: Decision-makers, translators and recipients

As illustrated in Figure 1, HQ 2 is sandwiched between corporate and regional headquarters, which creates a high level of duality (Chung *et al.*, 2011): talent management strategies must be rolled out as intended by corporate but fit into the regional-level context. Consequently, corporate executives from HQ 2, namely the CEO, vice presidents and general managers, are key *decision-makers* in translating the strategic choices made by HQH. Once HQ 2 has embedded global HQH policies in its own corporate strategies, including talent management, RH office members then translate these corporate ideas into practices at the subsidiary (HC and RB) level. Consequently, RH executives and middle-level managers are key *translators* of the strategic choices coming from HQ 2. We term these *translators* rather than *decision-makers* because of the extent to which they focus on the realities of implementation at the local level, ensuring fit and responsiveness. These regional offices are influenced not only by the input of external stakeholders but also by corporate HQ, host country offices and local regional businesses. The RB level is ABC's core business and includes employees who have been working in the mining operations for many years, building tacit knowledge and developing strong relationships. Of HQ 2's 30,000 employees and contractors in Peru, Chile and Argentina in 2011, about 85% were located in the RBs, predominantly at the rank of operator. Superintendents and supervisors (line managers and non-management personnel) are responsible for overseeing the operators' work, and therefore play a critical role as both *recipients* of corporate strategies, as well as re-translating these strategies to lower levels in the organization, including other professionals, administrators and importantly operators at site level. Figure 2 summarizes the key actors in talent management strategy translation from corporate to subsidiaries in ABC.

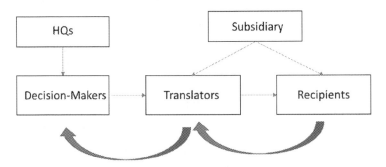

Figure 2.   Key actors in strategy translation from corporate to subsidiaries

Source: Based on Beamond *et al.* (2019).

Talent management strategy challenges

Against this organizational backdrop, the decision-makers, translators and recipients faced a number of challenges related to talent management, among which five emerged as core, as we detail further here.

Work motivation, satisfaction and loyalty

Although 80% of interviewees indicated high work motivation and 20% medium, this varied somewhat across mine sites. The possible causes of variation may be the proximity of the mine to other prosperous mines, housing sites and facilities. For example, interviewees from one site, although highly motivated, also expressed a high degree of stress due to the uncertainties of the business at the time. Changes in business management, the potential sale of the business, reduction of staff and demands of production rates from management contributed to raise anxiety.

Levels of satisfaction at work varied across mining operations, but most reported being either satisfied or very satisfied. However, the meaning of "satisfaction" does not necessarily refer to the workplace and/or managerial practices. Most of the interviewees, particularly among the translator and recipient groups, reported their level of work satisfaction in relation to their work activities or the company and to a sense of pride for the organization: "Almost all of them [who worked in this mining operation] have been there since the start of this operation and they wear the shirt [means a sense of belonging] of [the mining operation's name]" (Manager in a mining operation). Interviewees were asked to indicate which of the following elements was most important to improving their work: increasing salary, quality of life, capacity-building programs, promotion, recognition and mobility. The findings are presented in Figure 3, whereby it can be seen that, "quality of life" was most preferred, followed by "recognition", "promotion", "mobility" and "capacity building". The element with fewest responses was "increasing salary".

Interviewees were also asked to respond with one word as to what "loyalty to a company" means to them (not necessarily loyalty to ABC). The first seven words mentioned are illustrated in Figure 4: "commitment" and "recognition" stand out, followed by "sense of affection", "sense of inclusion", "sense of gratefulness", "sense of satisfaction", and "opportunities". The commitment expressed by translator and recipient interviewees referred to emotional attachment to, identification with and

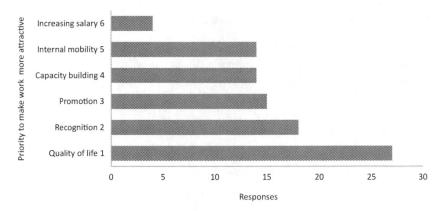

Figure 3.   Work priorities as reported by interviewees

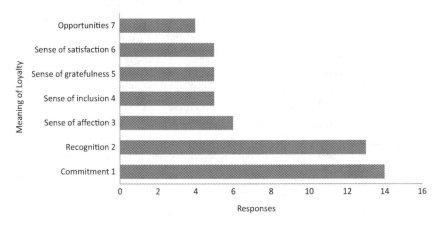

Figure 4.   The meaning of "Loyalty to a Company" according to interviewees

involvement in the organization. Again, recognition is extremely important to employees: "The Company is like my son. I have known it since it was born" (Supervisor).

Employee turnover

Opinions on employee turnover levels varied considerably among interviewees. Based on their knowledge, while the decision-maker group's answers related to the activity of the whole of the Latin America business, answers from translator and recipient groups located in mining operations related to local turnover where they worked. In general, decision-makers saw turnover levels as low and the others as medium to high. High turnover was attributed to various factors at the local level including: a lack of managerial skills and recognition; bureaucratic corporate salary policies; better salary packages from competitors, especially for people who had received training; the FIFO operation (as indicated in previous studies that workforce turnover in FIFO sites tend to reach a higher level of turnover than those closer to towns: Beach *et al.*, 2003); family reasons; discontentment with workplace practices; and the mining lifestyle. "There is not skill shortage as what we have in Australia" (Corporate General Manager HR). "The corporate area of ABC has unrealistic expectations because they were told there is not a high turnover rate, when in fact there is" (Superintendent). A common observation about turnover across interviewees was related to impact: when key employees, who hold important technical and/or process knowledge of a particular area, leave the company, this creates more problems than when a whole group of less knowledgeable workers leave. High performers with key tacit technical knowledge were particularly problematic if they left, as finding an appropriate replacement or training someone in comparable skills would typically take a minimum of 2 years. Problems incurred included reduced productivity, stress on other workers, fatigue due to increased overtime requirements, loss of industry-specific experience and project development and production delays. Counter to the issue of turnover among key high performers, there was the opposite problem of a substantial percentage of staff with low productivity staying in the company. One mine had a very low employee turnover rate. This was good in terms of talent retention; however, it was also causing a sense of monotony among employees who were unable to advance their professional career. Nevertheless, pride in the mine was high as many ABC executives came from this mining operation. They had a particularly strong positive sentiment toward the current CEO, respecting him not only for his managerial practices but also for his humanistic approach toward managing Latin Americans. Nevertheless, there was a negative perception toward the human resource department: "They [corporate] need to make the human resources department more humanized. When they transmit corporate polices and business strategies they need to take into consideration the different intellectual levels that may be present in the subsidiaries, take the countries culture and the regional culture into consideration" (Supervisor). In general, the turnover rate did not necessarily reflect its level of impact.

The mine with the lowest turnover nevertheless found it very difficult to find professionals in the market with appropriate skills when a key performer left the mine. This issue is acute when, culturally speaking, some countries are more protective of their own talent, which restricts the possibility of using temporary skilled migration across the region. Some HR interviewees expressed the feeling of pressure being put on them because of these turnover issues that conflicted with corporate strategic targets and the different views in relation to percentages of turnover: "I would say that our turnover level is low and it really depends on your cultural reference point. For example, in Australia our turnover is 40%, where 20 percent is low. In Peru our turnover is four or five percent which I think is very low, but our Peruvian counterparts would say it's very high" (Executive of HR).

Attracting, selecting, developing and retaining talent

The reported challenges associated with talent management in terms of attracting, selecting, developing and retaining talent focused primarily on five issues: a company's lack of career path initiatives, a lack of effective training to develop local talent, a lack of a sense of ownership of talent development, a lack of a sense of inclusion within the firm, and a lack of corporate brand promotion to attract talent. Focusing on local talent, most superintendents, supervisors (translators and recipients) and high-level personnel (decision-makers) were aware of the existence of local talent development strategies, however, around one-quarter of them were not. As with employee turnover, decision-makers tended to discuss local talent with reference to the whole company, whereas interviewees from mining operations (recipients) referred to the region where their mining operation was located. Development was focused on a range of issues from training local contractors on corporate policies, including safety, to community relations programs for regional women and training women to successfully operate heavy machinery (although there was no formal capacity-building program to attract and retain women to occupy positions in the company). The structure of programs focused on regional talent (indigenous and/or people from rural communities) was mainly created and developed by each area of the mining operation in accordance with their needs. These programs were financially and logistically supported by HR departments. As an example, one operation had its own training budget and program focused on its needs and those of the regional people ("comuneros"), as they represent a large number of employees: "In this area, 60% of the employees come from the communities or Comuneros" (Superintended on a mining operation). Following the success of this program, it was implemented across other areas by the HR department. The training of "comuneros" from the areas surrounding the mine operations encourages recruitment and retention among indigenous people, which had been a challenge: meal times, community commitments and family land traditions are some of the cultural challenges that mentors face.

Capacity-building programs

Although 75% of interviewees reported having undertaken capacity-building programs organized by the company, many commented on the lack of access to such programs, either due to requiring management approval or a lack of awareness of the availability of training. For example, when asked if interviewees knew about the corporate "talent pool" program, one of ABC's most important talent management programs, most of them did not know about it, including some superintendents, supervisors and lower level employees. Some respondents declared: "I have heard about it but I'm not sure if it [talent pool] exists." "It is an important program from Australia that does not work here" (Superintendent HR). All interviewees expressed strong interest in capacity building, particularly in postgraduate programs, as they saw that this would advance their professional careers. Many interviewees also indicated that (particularly single) employees were keen to participate in internships at other national or international mining operations and that such internships could be part of the capacity-building training to improve their abilities. The effect of capacity building for motivation, performance, satisfaction, loyalty and corporate social responsibility (CSR) at work was also important to interviewees, particularly performance and CSR. According to interviewees, those who received the most training and had the most knowledge also demonstrated the highest performance levels. For the translator and recipient groups, CSR relates to the capacity of the organization to provide training to people in the communities in which the mine is operating. Staff see this as a very positive link with communities, leading to retention. Nevertheless, most interviewees across the three groups (decision-makers, translators and recipients) declared that although capacity-building programs were important for talent retention, these programs could not guarantee loyalty to the company.

Alignment between HRM and business strategies

In general, alignment between the strategic business plan and HRM strategies was considered average to good. The two most dominant opinions included the decision-makers' perception that corporate strategies were directly interconnected with HRM strategies, while translators and recipients expressed some concerns over this alignment: "The salary policies come from Australia, but they should not implement the same policies from Australia in [the mining operation name] due to our differences" (Superintendent). Some of the comments exposed the perceived difference between the theory of alignment and its practice, with great satisfaction expressed regarding the corporation's pillars of sustainable development, but little awareness of the pillars being reflected in practice. "[it is] about sustainability which means working together for the future of the community and the company (Executive)." "There is a lack of community conscience. It means that ABC [corporate] lacks of consciousness about the fact that staff are part of the community. They are also the community" (Superintendent). Most of the mining operations expressed slight to moderate dissatisfaction with the HRM strategies, specifically regarding the high rate of turnover of high performers and the subsequent difficulty in finding the right talent with appropriate technical and managerial skills. It was also felt that alignment between the corporate and HRM strategies could be stronger in terms of planning for future talent needs to develop current and future projects, retention packages and structured capacity-building programs. Related to changing talent demographics, less than one-quarter of interviewees was aware of a corporate strategy to address this. Although there was a succession plan in place, it did not include strategies to specifically address demographics, instead focusing on preparing key employees to take over positions in the business but with no planned tacit knowledge transfer from employees approaching retirement. Key characteristics of core talent management challenges are illustrated in Table 3.

Table 3. Key characteristics of core talent management challenges

Core talent management challenges	Key characteristics	Key aspects
Work motivation, satisfaction and loyalty	• Levels of satisfaction at work varied across mining operations • Key aspects for retention: Key aspects for loyalty: quality of life and recognition "Commitment" and "recognition"	• Meaning of satisfaction: affinity with work activities, affection toward the company and a sense of pride for the organization
Employee turnover	• Different perception on employee turnover among the three key actors: Translators and Recipients: high; Decision-Makers: not high	• High pressure levels: turnover by key talent with specific skills affecting corporate strategic targets
Challenges to attracting, selecting, developing, and retaining talent	• Lack of: career path initiatives; effective training to develop local talent; sense of ownership of talent development; sense of inclusion within the firm; corporate brand promotion to attract talent; training programs for women	• Different perception on local talent development strategies among key actors: translators and recipients: most of them were not aware of the strategy; decision-makers: aware as they developed the strategy • Influence of regional sections' training initiatives on the HR department
Importance of capacity-building programs	• Strong interest on: capacity building; work experience in other national or international mining operations • To key actors: Strong focus on relationship between CSR and capacity building for communities	• High effect of capacity building on motivation, performance, satisfaction, loyalty and corporate social responsibility • Capacity-building programs may not guarantee loyalty
Alignment between HR and business strategies	• Different perception between the three key actors: decision-Makers: high; translators and recipients: not high	• High level of dissatisfaction with HRM strategies due to turnover of high performers, and skill shortage

What Can We Learn from the ABC Case?

ABC operates in a dynamic market, influenced by the globalization of economies and a tightening supply of talent. Consequently, ABC must not only translate corporate talent management strategies effectively into all levels of the organization but also focus on global labor market challenges. If a subsidiary has a shortage of local talent, this shortage affects the company's overall performance. In this case study, we identified the core talent management challenges ABC faced in Latin America in the eyes of the key agents in the translation process. At a structural level, a corporate holding model of a mining MNE, such as ABC, has operations and headquarters that span multiple geographies. While mining operations are either open pits or underground, situated in the mountains or desert, and either isolated or close to communities, the regional HQ and host country offices are mainly located in principal cities. Moreover, although the inhabitants of most Latin American countries speak Spanish, their cultural diversity varies from one country to another. Differences within each country are also present, particularly between cities and remote regions. Consequently, an MNE's operations can be affected by both global factors and country-specific factors, including labor and environmental regulations, workforce qualifications, licenses to operate, community relations and cultural aspects (Jara *et al.*, 2010). The process of translating and communicating the corporate strategy into talent management practices in subsidiaries and mining operations, while being aware of such exogenous factors, is one of the foremost talent management challenges for academics and practitioners alike. The analysis of the structural level reveals complexities when translating corporate strategies to subsidiaries in emerging economies. In the ABC case, the key actors tasked with this translation process were located across multiple levels with three key roles: decision-making, translating and receiving. The decision-makers were in the holding company's headquarters, developing and exporting the talent management strategies for use across the organization's operations. The translators were predominantly in the regional headquarters, playing a crucial role in balancing the holding company's headquarters demands with the needs of regional offices and businesses. The recipients were the people working in the subsidiaries, either in host country offices or regional mining operations. Each actor played an essential role in the translation process from the top to the bottom of the company and in feeding essential information from the bottom to the top to facilitate translation. As key actors to the action of translation, regional executives were influenced from top (corporate HQ), they also were influenced by bottom (local country offices and regional business) levels. Hence, local responses to corporate strategies were shaped by interpretations and perceptions of the strategy, which were molded by institutional and relational contexts in the organization (Kostova & Roth, 2002). Findings illustrated that whereas the CEO showed strong humanistic characteristics (Elvira & Davila, 2005) as valued by the Latin Americans, most of the HR personnel were not viewed as humanistic supporters at the service of workers, but a threat (Elvira & Davila, 2005). Findings disclosed different perceptions between decision-makers and translators/recipients, confirming that when ideas and practices move ideas move from one context (corporate) to another (subsidiary) they are changed through the process of transference and transformation (Czarniawska & Sevon, 2005).

Overall, the study identified five core interrelated themes related to talent management challenges. Motivation, satisfaction and loyalty are related to employees feeling an affinity with work activities, affection toward the company and a sense of company pride. Motivation relates to public recognition for high performance and promotion (Sully De Luque & Arbaiza, 2005) and the organization's commitment to employees through work security, training and development and humanistic policies (Davila & Elvira, 2012). The latter involves training programs for employees and their families, transparency, good working conditions, and in general, a state of health, safety and quality of life (Perez Arrau *et al.*, 2012; Sully *et al.*, 2005). This type of motivation not only increases employee loyalty but also enhances the organization's reputation for corporate ethics, social responsibility and altruism (Davila & Elvira, 2012). The meaning of motivation and satisfaction demonstrated in the case is highly interrelated with paternalistic values and, therefore, to retention. Traditionally, Latin America has been characterized by paternalism, with firms having a benevolent attitude toward employees, caring and protecting behavior and understanding employees' (and their families') best interests (Perez Arrau *et al.*, 2012). This creates psychological and social contracts between superiors and subordinates: "in which person-centered management should take preeminence over merely profit-centered goals" (Davila & Elvira, 2012, p. 549). Nowadays, although paternalism is still embedded in many countries (Perez Arrau *et al.*, 2012), the region is moving from paternalism to performance-driven practices, creating hybrid HRM practices with the aim of organizations balancing global orientation and localization (Elvira & Davila, 2005). This explains why findings reveal the importance of two core challenges to attracting, selecting, developing and retaining talent: capacity-building programs to advance in employee careers and feeling loyalty toward the organization and ownership. Both are significant to attracting and retaining local key talent in the region and therefore to achieving sustainable competitive advantage. The findings from interviewees regarding their perceptions of what made their work attractive were in line with other consultancy research findings. Deloitte (2011) found that "what employees are saying is quite simple: Money is important, but greater compensation alone is not enough to keep them satisfied in their jobs". This case study shows that increasing salary was no longer the main factor in recruiting and retaining staff. In fact, quality of life contributes substantially to an employee's decision to stay with or leave an organization. Employees who knew that they were appreciated and valued for their work demonstrated lower employee turnover. Finally, this case study reveals the importance of alignment between HRM and business strategies. Although this study demonstrated alignment to a certain extent between HRM and the business, it was also noted that whereas the CEO showed strong humanistic characteristics as valued by the Latin Americans (Elvira & Davila, 2005), most of the HR personnel were not viewed as humanistic advocates at the service of employees but instead as a threat. Alignment of strategies is, of course, important, but perhaps even more so the values behind the strategies across the organization also need to align to create an appropriate corporate culture.

Conclusion

The ABC case study highlights how talent management strategies of MNEs with operations in emerging economies may need to adapt to complex local factors that influence the motivation, satisfaction and loyalty of local talent. There is, however, a concurrent need to adopt corporate headquarters' strategies across all organizational levels through a process of translation, responding to both globalization and localization needs simultaneously. MNEs with operations in emerging economies need to work on strategies that cover local talent skills shortages, retention strategies and increasing competition for valuable talent. Future research on globalization trends that affect talent management strategies is therefore required to inform knowledge and practice in this field.

References

Beach, R., Brereton, D. & Cliff, D. (2003). *Workforce Turnover in FIFO Mining Operations in Australia: An Exploratory Study*. Centre for Social Responsibility in Mining, Sustainable Minerals Institute, University of Queensland, Queensland, Australia.

Beamond, M., Farndale, E. & Hartel, C. (2016). MNE translation of corporate talent management strategies to subsidiaries in emerging economies. *Journal of World Business,* 51, 499–510.

Beamond, M., Farndale, E. & Hartel, C. (2019). Frames and actors: Translating talent management strategy to Latin America. *Management and Organization Review,* 16(2), 1–38.

Bonache, J., Trullen, J. & Sanchez, J.I. (2012). Managing cross-cultural differences: Testing human resource models in Latin America. *Journal of Business Research,* 65, 1773–1781.

Braun, V., & Clarke, V. (2006). Using thematic analysis in psychology. *Qualitative Research in Psychology,* 3(2), 77–101.

Chung, C., Bozkurt, Ö. & Sparrow, P. (2012). Managing the duality of IHRM: Unravelling the strategy and perceptions of key actors in South Korean MNCs. *The International Journal of Human Resource Management,* 23(11), 2333–2353.

Czarniawska, B. & Sevon, G. (2005). *Global Ideas: How Ideas, Objects and Practices Travel in the Global Economy*. Sweden and Norway/Liber and Copenhagen: Business School Press.

Davila, A. & Elvira, M.M. (2012). Humanistic leadership: Lessons from Latin America. *Journal of World Business,* 47(4), 548–554.

Deloitte (2011). Talent Edge 2020: Building the recovery together. What talent expects and how leaders are responding. Retrieved from: https://dupress.deloitte.com/dup-us-en/topics/talent/talent-edge-2020-building-the-recovery-together.html [Accessed on March 2020].

Elvira, M.M. & Davila, A. (2005). Emergent directions for human resource management research in Latin America. *International Journal of Human Resources Management,* 16(12), 2265–2282.

Graebner, M.E., Martin, J.A. & Roundy, P.T. (2012). Qualitative data: Cooking without a recipe. *Strategic Organization,* 10(3), 276–284.

Illes, P., Chuai, X. & Preece, D. (2010). Talent management in multinational companies in Beijing: Definitions, differences and drivers. *Journal of World Business,* 45(2), 179–189.

IMF. (2017). World Economic Outlook. International Monetary Fund. Retrieved from:http://www.imf.org/en/publications/weo/issues/2017/04/04/world-economic-outlook-april-2017 [Accessed on March 2020].

Jara, J.J., Perez, P. & Villalobos, P. (2010). Good deposits are not enough: Mining labor productivity analysis in the copper industry in Chile and Peru 1992–2009. *Resources Policy*, 35(4), 247–256.

Kostova, T. & Roth, K. (2002). Adoption of an organizational practice by subsidiaries of multinational corporations: Institutional and relational. *The Academy of Management Journal*, 45(1), 215–233.

Latukha, M. (2016). *Talent management in emerging market firms: Global strategy and local challenges*. London, UK: Palgrave Macmillan.

Li, S. & Scullion H. (2010). Developing the local competence of expatriate managers for emerging economies: A knowledge-based approach. *Journal of World Business*, 45(2), 190–196.

Meyers, M.C. & Van Woerkom, M. (2014). The influence of underlying philosophies on talent management: Theory, implications for practice, and research agenda. *Journal of World Business*, 49, 192–203.

Patton, M. (1990). *Qualitative Evaluation and Research Methods*. Beverly Hills, CA: Sage.

Perez Arrau, G., Eades, E. & Wilson, J. (2012). Managing human resources in the Latin American context: The case of Chile. *The International Journal of Human Resource Management*, 23(15), 3133–3150.

Sully, De Luque, M.F. & Arbaiza, L.A. (2005). The complexity of managing human resources in Peru. *The International Journal of Human Resource Management*, 16(12), 2237–2253.

Tarique, I. & Schuler, R.S. (2010). Global talent management: Literature review, integrative framework, and suggestions for further research. *Journal of World Business*, 45(2), 122–133.

Tymon, W.G., Stumpf, S.A. & Doh, J.P. (2010). Exploring talent management in India: The neglected role of intrinsic rewards. *Journal of World Business*, 45(2), 109–121.

Wright, P.M., McMahan, G.C. & McWilliams, A. (1994). Human resources and sustained competitive advantage: A resource-based perspective. *The International Journal of Human Resource Management*, 5, 301–326.

Wright M., Filatotchev I., Hoskisson R.E. & Peng, M.W. (2005). Guest editors' introduction strategy research in emerging economies: Challenging the conventional wisdom. *Journal of Management Studies*, 42, 1–33.

Yin, R.K. (2017). *Case Study Research and Applications: Design and Methods*. Beverly Hills, CA: Sage.

Chapter 8

The Impact of an Incubation Process on Management Control Systems of Start-Ups

Miguel Angel Gil Robles[*] and Hanna Klarner

Tecnológico de Monterrey, Tecnológico, 64849 Monterrey, N.L., Mexico Reutlingen University, 72762 Reutlingen, Germany

[*]*m.gil@tec.mx*

Management control systems (MCSs) and business incubators (BIs) are both argued to support start-ups in their survival and growth. This research links these two increasingly relevant topics in literature and aims at answering the research question: How does an incubation process affect MCSs in start-ups? A qualitative and exploratory case study is used to answer the research question. Semi-structured interviews were conducted with three start-ups and the management of the Mexican incubator "TecLean". The findings of this research suggest that an incubation process influences the development of MCSs in start-ups in at least two ways. First, an incubation process pushes the start-ups toward a non-traditional conceptualization of MCSs to include their stakeholders' perspective. Second, an incubation process highlights the relevance of MCSs when aiming at obtaining venture capital (VC) and thus increases the start-ups' awareness and initiative to implement stricter MCSs. This research suggests that practitioners in BIs should teach start-ups consciously on how to design MCSs. This may increase start-ups' access to VC.

Introduction

Merchant and van der Stede (2017) define a management control system (MCS) as the collection of control mechanisms used by managers to ensure the behaviors and decisions of their employees are consistent with the organization's objectives and strategies. As such, MCSs are commonly argued to improve performance in large or medium-sized organizations (Coyte, 2019; Diefenbach *et al.*, 2018; Junqueira *et al.*, 2016). However, the contribution of MCSs in start-ups has been a controversial topic. Early streams of literature focus on the trade-off between innovation and control, concluding that formal MCSs are hindering the capabilities of start-ups (Knight, 1967; Pierce & Delbecq, 1977). More recent studies have found that MCSs benefit innovation by providing relevant information (Davila, 2000) and that MCSs are a prerequisite for a start-up's growth and survival (Davila & Foster, 2007; Davila *et al.*, 2010). Business incubators (BIs) aim at creating successful new organizations (Hackett & Dilts, 2004). A commonly accepted assumption is that BIs teach start-ups important management skills (Bruneel *et al.*, 2012). The accounting literature argues that resulting MCSs are essential for the survival of a start-up (Davila & Foster, 2007; Davila *et al.*, 2010). However, it has not been investigated how BIs may impact start-ups' MCSs. Therefore, this research will aim at answering the research question, how does an incubation process affect MCSs in start-ups? A qualitative, exploratory case study is used to answer the research question. Semi-structured interviews were conducted with managers and three start-ups of the BI *TecLean* closely tied to the Mexican university — *Instituto Tecnológico y de Estudios Superiores de Monterrey* (ITESM). This research concludes that an incubation process is a further external factor impacting the MCSs within start-ups. This research argues that the BI pushes the start-ups toward a non-traditional conceptualization of MCSs to include their stakeholders' perspective. This research finds that an incubation process highlights the relevance of MCSs to obtain VC financing. It thus increases the start-ups' awareness and initiative to implement stronger MCSs. Therefore, the concrete plan to apply for VC may already be a driver toward the adoption of MCSs.

Literature Review

MCSs in Start-Ups

Traditionally, MCSs were conceptualized as a type of accounting system (Lowe, 1971). However, this view has changed over time (Lowe, 1971; Todd, 1977). Literature still does not provide an absolute definition of MCSs, but researchers have acknowledged their interdisciplinary nature (Malmi & Brown, 2008). Apart from formal financial mechanisms, administrative or cultural elements are argued to be equally important in the design of an MCS (Malmi & Brown, 2008). Merchant and van der Stede (2017), for example, use a behavioral approach and define an MCS as the collection of control mechanisms used by managers to ensure the behaviors and decisions of their employees are consistent with the organization's objectives and strategies. Similarly, Collins (1982) focuses on controlling employees' role behavior and motivation. Simons (1995) argues that MCSs are implemented for maintaining and altering organizational behavior. Other studies focus more broadly on the accomplishment of goals and strategy implementation (Cunningham, 1992). Although concrete definitions differ widely, researchers have agreed that MCSs are a combination of various interrelated mechanisms within an organization and not just a single practice that operates in isolation (Malmi & Brown, 2008; Merchant & van der Stede, 2017; Strauss *et al.*, 2013). Merchant and van der Stede (2017) argue that the MCS of every organization includes a combination of four systems (action, results, personnel and cultural) but that this combination can vary due to different organizational needs. Cunningham (1992) suggests a broader but very similar division (results control and behavioral control).

The accounting literature argues that MCSs are beneficial for mature organizations in terms of performance, effectiveness and competitive advantages (Coyte, 2019; Diefenbach *et al.*, 2018; Junqueira *et al.*, 2016). For start-ups, however, the implementation of MCSs has been discussed controversially. A start-up can be defined as an organization in the birth stage (Miller & Friesen, 1984; Samagaio *et al.*, 2018). Start-ups are commonly associated with innovativeness (e.g. Freeman & Engel, 2007) and are often characterized by the domination of their owners and the absence of formal systems in general (Miller & Friesen, 1984). Early streams of literature regarding MCSs and start-ups focus on the trade-off between innovation and control. Such studies argue that formal MCSs are hindering the capabilities of start-ups (Knight, 1967; Pierce & Delbecq, 1977).

On the contrary, more recent literature has found conflicting results. The growth of an organization is characterized by increased complexity in decision-making (Miller & Friesen, 1984). In a very early stage, a start-up may operate effectively when it is primarily dominated by its owner who takes all decisions. However, with increasing size, this centralized decision-making can quickly become too costly due to its time intensity and related administrative challenges (Davila & Foster, 2007). Thus, implementing MCSs enables managers to control the start-up more effectively and provides managers with the necessary information to make better business decisions (Davila *et al.*, 2015). Therefore, MCSs can be seen as a prerequisite for the growth of a start-up (Davila, 2000; Davila *et al.*, 2015). On the contrary, a start-up's refusal to implement MCSs can ultimately lead to its failure (Davila *et al.*, 2010).

Davila (2000) suggests that going beyond financial measures in MCSs is especially crucial for start-ups. This is consistent with the framework of Merchant and van der Stede (2017), suggesting that non-financial measures form a big part of MCSs and that the composition of MCSs can vary widely between different organizations. Therefore, in the following, a comprehensive framework of MCSs will be applied. This research will focus on all types of internal systems or routines, formal and informal, that start-ups implement to achieve their organization's goals. This chapter adopts the more contemporary notion of MCSs which argues that control is achieved by influencing the behavior of organizational members (Mechant & van der Stede, 2017) by incorporating quantitative and qualitative mechanisms. By adopting this definition of MCSs, this chapter assumes that the objective of managerial control in start-ups is to guide organizational members to complete stated objectives (Davila & Foster, 2007). Through the three case studies, this chapter finds the relationship that exists between the incubation process and the resulting MCSs.

Business Incubators and Incubation Processes

Innovation is argued to be a significant factor in fostering regional economic growth (Autio *et al.*, 2018; Schramm, 2004; Torres-Preciado *et al.*, 2014). Since start-ups are commonly associated with innovativeness (e.g. Freeman & Engel, 2007), policymakers, universities and other actors increasingly aim at providing the necessary infrastructure, in the form of BIs, for their survival and growth (Autio *et al.*, 2018; Mian *et al.*, 2016; Rubin *et al.*, 2015). Hackett and Dilts (2004) suggest that a BI is a shared office space facility, which provides an intervention system of monitoring and business assistance to its incubated start-ups. Business assistance commonly takes the form of shared support services and mentoring by professionals (Bergek & Norrman, 2008). Additionally, the network that BIs provide is a critical part of their offering, connecting start-ups to venture capitalists, professionals and other entrepreneurs (Hackett & Dilts, 2004). Business assistance for start-ups is argued to be advantageous since new entrepreneurs often lack crucial management skills. Such skills often determine whether an organization will survive its first years of business. *Learning by doing* is possible, but it is often associated with higher cost and time intensity. Providing business assistance through BIs may, therefore, significantly accelerate the learning process in new ventures and increase survival rates (Bruneel *et al.*, 2012).

MCSs in Start-Ups and the Incubation Process

Previous studies on MCSs in start-ups have investigated several factors influencing their adoption (Davila, 2000; Davila *et al.*, 2015). Davila *et al.* (2010) argue that systems are adopted proactively or reactively: proactively when the management team has the relevant knowledge to introduce MCSs themselves, or reactively when the start-up has experienced problems related to their personal management style. Apart from these factors, studies acknowledge that external factors may influence the adoption of MCSs more than previously assumed (Davila, 2000). Such studies have focused on Legitimization or Contracting and VC as external factors (Davila *et al.*, 2010). Venture capitalists can require the formalization of companies and, thus, the implementation of MCSs (Granlund & Taipaleenmäki, 2005). These are perceived as being valuable since venture capitalists may have previously experienced that start-ups with weak or no MCSs are failing. Start-ups with more formal systems are thus subject to higher company valuation by venture capitalists (Davila *et al.*, 2015).

Even though BIs are widely recognized to teach start-ups essential management skills (Bruneel *et al.*, 2012), and they are gaining importance in theory and practice (Bergek & Norrman, 2008), it has not been investigated how they can influence the MCSs in start-ups. Both BIs and MCSs can aid the survival of start-ups and therefore foster economic growth in developing countries such as Mexico; thus, it is highly relevant to explore this gap in the literature. In accordance with Alvesson and Sandberg

(2011), this research is also relevant, since it problematizes the definition of MCSs in the existing literature and opts for broadening the framework in which MCSs are applied.

Methodology

As argued in the previous section, MCSs remain challenging to conceptualize (Malmi & Brown, 2008). Exploratory research is appropriate when conceptualization is difficult and when the context and the phenomenon are closely interrelated (Saunders *et al.*, 2016). Qualitative Research has gained increasing attention in Management Accounting literature (Lee & Humphrey, 2006) since it can explore social phenomena such as MCSs in-depth (Ahrens & Chapman, 2006). Consequently, this research is qualitative and exploratory. It follows the outline of a horizontal case study, as suggested by Yin (2018), to answer research questions that are concerned with how or why a phenomenon occurs.

The data were collected from the BI *TecLean* at the Mexican university ITESM, Campus Guadalajara. It includes a sample of three start-ups within the incubator, as well as the incubator's management. Semi-structured interviews were selected as the primary method to collect data. While the underlying structure in semi-structured interviews increases the comparability of the answers between the start-ups (Scapens, 2004), such interviews remain flexible and allow to adjust the questions depending on the interviewees' responses (Bryman & Bell, 2007). The interviews were recorded and transcribed. In total, the researchers completed 29 interviews in the period between May and September 2019. The interviewees included senior managers, employees, freelancers and incubator officers.

The data from each case were first investigated separately by re-reading transcripts several times and then highlighting and color-coding the important topics (Eisenhardt, 1989; Quinlan *et al.*, 2015). Diagrams were used as a tool to further illustrate the relationship between the relevant variables (Scapens, 2004) and to further analyze the data. Various measures have been taken to ensure data validity. Authenticity and plausibility of the Data Analysis are two central elements of validation in Management Accounting Research. Consequently, participants from different levels within the incubator were interviewed, and the collected data were triangulated to obtain a complete and logical picture of the cases

(Yin, 2018). The consideration of various perspectives within the incubator aimed at giving a thick description of the incubator and the MCSs (Lukka & Modell, 2010). Lastly, reliability was ensured by developing a case study protocol and maintaining a chain of evidence (Yin, 2018).

The Cases

Background

TecLean is a BI based in Guadalajara, Mexico, closely tied to the university ITESM. Its goal is to facilitate the creation of successful, technology-based, start-ups. The director of the incubator, Yenira, explains: "Its goal is to foster the creation of start-ups, technology-based start-ups, what we define like technology-based is that it has innovation, that it develops or adopts technology, that it can scale and that it has a positive impact to the society." The incubator offers three programs: TecLean Discovery, TecLean Launch and TecLean Growth. The first program focuses on developing a start-up's idea with the Design Thinking methodology. The second program aims at validating an idea or a minimal viable product with the Lean start-up methodology. The last program assists the start-ups in growing their businesses after having launched the product. To be considered for the program, applicants have to complete a form containing general information about their start-up, and during a selection day, the entrepreneurs have to pitch their idea to a committee consisting of persons from TecLean and ITESM. The central criterion for acceptance is that start-ups have a technology innovation process. Their industries differ widely.

Incubation Process

TecLean's key offerings during the incubation process include a free co-working space at ITESM, mentoring, direct contact to experts and networking. Furthermore, start-ups can participate in workshops with professionals from the technology sector and they can grow their team with students from ITESM or pitch their idea to ITESM to become a supplier, benefitting both parties. First, selected start-ups are analyzed by a team of the incubator regarding the five areas Team, Business, Market, Product and Finance. A mentoring board with experts from ITESM and external parties is formed. The board defines key focus areas and establishes a plan for the start-ups on how to improve these identified issues. The program coordinator then monitors the progress in weekly meetings with the start-ups and questions their recent achievements. Feedback is provided, and the information is collected in a database. The program coordinator Abraham explains: "The key focus is the growth with the analysis of all the strategies. The gold asset that we offer at the growth program is that they have about 24 personal meetings with mentors. And at the end of the program [they] have a lot of enrichment for their start-ups because they had the opportunity to talk with experienced people from the Business Ecosystem." The three start-ups Start-up A, Start-up B and Start-up C were investigated during the case study. To facilitate cross-case analysis, the MCSs were categorized as the ones developed by own initiative and others that were developed as a result of the incubation process. The second aspect considered was whether the MCSs were implemented with or without TecLean's help. While these categories emerged from empirical data, this division considers reviewed literature in so far, as it divides the implementation of MCSs according to external and internal factors (Davila *et al.*, 2010).

Start-Up A

Start-up A is a Mexican start-up, based in the city of Guadalajara, which was founded in 2018. It operates a website with deals of restaurants and bars close to the users' location. Start-up A generates income by selling monthly subscriptions to restaurants that want to publish their deals. Start-up A, at a very early stage, participated in a governmental incubation program, Reto Zapopan. It then has participated in the program TecLean Growth. Start-up A has four employees. While the founder and simultaneous director focuses on administration, his employees work in the areas of marketing, media, merchandising and sales. Start-up A does not have any external investors but has concrete plans to apply for VC. As argued in the previous sections, the systems within Start-up A's MCS are categorized according to the factors influencing the initiative and implementation. Start-up A has implemented one system with three mechanisms by its own initiative and without TecLean's help. The start-up has set up monthly and weekly performance targets in the areas of sales, social media and merchandise to track its improvement. The performance of its employees is measured by investigating whether previously set objectives had been accomplished. A cash budget was implemented due to previously experienced problems with high expenses within the organization. The director argues: "we were spending a lot of money without actually putting any limits to it or having any structure that was something that came from inside the company. I almost did everything by myself. I didn't ask them [TecLean] for help in that area actually." Start-up A implemented one element of its MCS internally after suggestion from TecLean. The software *Coophi* is used as a checklist and for task management. It was recommended by a mentor from the incubator who was working with this software. The director decided to use Coophi to ensure that tasks were completed by his employees. He states: "One of my mentors was also working with this company, which is also a Mexican start-up from Guadalajara. It really does help a lot in management and to making sure things are getting done in your company". The implementation of three elements within its MCS was initiated by the director but supported by TecLean. Start-up A established a sales forecast with TecLean's help to create budgets in different departments. The director describes: "[W]hen we actually made a forecast, we could see how much money we were expecting to make each month, so that way, we could put a budget. I wanted to do it, and they [TecLean] helped me make it happen." Likewise, return on investment (ROI) is measured in the departments that manage money for better decision-making. Bonuses serve as an incentive to the salespeople. Additionally, TecLean encouraged Start-up A to implement an organizational structure, as well as a variance analysis and supported it in doing so. The organizational structure was introduced for the division of labor between the departments. The variance analysis was created to analyze the forecasted targets. The director argues: "The Variance Analysis started about a month after we started with the forecasts, so because, well, that was when we started to be able to compare, you know? It's important for them also to know how we're doing, for the incubator". Finally, another element of Start-up A's MCS was encouraged by TecLean. Start-up A implemented, with the BI's help, external performance targets that are disclosed to the customers specifically. The director describes: "We give them an analysis on the performance of their different apps that they have in the platform. So, the incubator helped me design and decide which objectives and which parameters and which targets we're going to give the customers." In Start-up A's case, the director explained that he had seen many mechanisms during the previous incubation program. This drove his decision in how to compose Start-up A's

MCS and he, therefore, asked TecLean to support him in the implementation. The director's initiative was either fostered by problems that he had experienced in certain management areas of his start-up or by his proactive desire to make informed decisions. He summarizes: "The incubator like doesn't make you do anything, it's a lot of mentorship. What they really helped me was in making it happen. Like going from point A to point B."

Start-Up B

Start-up B is a Mexican start-up that was founded in 2016. It produces handmade leather collars for dogs and cats with artisanal beads typically used in Mexican indigenous art. The products are sold directly to customers or via distributors. Start-up B has just completed the program *TecLean Growth*. For bureaucratic and legal reasons, it has decided not to have formal employees. Therefore, it is regularly working with 11 freelancers. It does not have any investors, and the co-founders are not yet sure whether to apply for VC. Start-up B received 60,000 Mexican Pesos (MXN), equivalent to about 2,700 Euro (EUR), in government support (European Central Bank, 2019). The interview was conducted with one of the co-founders of the start-up. Start-up B has initiated the implementation of two elements within its MCS and was supported by TecLean in their implementation. Start-up B uses checklists for all stages of production of the collars. Start-up B has improved the checklists since their business is continually growing, posing logistical challenges. Furthermore, Start-up B uses concrete criteria for selecting their freelancers by asking them to provide sample products and then evaluating their quality. To describe the selection process, the founder states: "You can give me ten product[s], and you come here like at 8 AM, punctuality, responsibility and the ten product[s], perfect job. [TecLean] advise[s] us about how we can select." TecLean suggested that Start-up B implements legal contracts for its freelancing artists to ensure that they produce only for Start-up B. TecLean supported their design. The founder describes: "[TecLean] advise[s] us about the things that we have to do. For example, contracts, [since] the person who works with the leather, they can't do collar dogs for anyone." Start-up B has further introduced two systems that could not be further categorized due to a lack of information. As an example, Start-up B had created statements of mission and vision 5 years ago, before the start-up was founded. While in the beginning, the co-founder says that the incubator helped with the mission and vision, she then says they have not changed anything. She argues: "TecLean help[s] you to set down your idea, to plan very well what you want to do, what is your mission, what is your vision, we have it in five years, but I think that we have to make a more real statement of mission. I think that we are ready to redesign." Furthermore, Start-up B provides freelancing artists with courses in legal and financial matters and enabled one of their artists to finish her high school degree. However, it remains unclear why and how exactly Start-up B has introduced these benefits. It becomes evident that Start-up B has focused on operational issues, mainly the delivery to its clients. Therefore, it has implemented only a few formal systems. TecLean had helped Start-up B especially in situations, in which problems occurred, and its mentors guided their attention toward problematic areas. The founder seems to be aware of a lack of internal procedures; she argues: "That kind of things, we have to work more about, inside the company. But, in this moment that we have many clients we have to answer, you know? Yeah, priorities".

Start-Up C

Start-up C is a Mexican start-up in the biotechnology industry that sells a probiotic smoothie. Its idea was developed in 2015, initially as a side project during the co-founders' studies. Currently, Start-up C does not have any formal employees but works with freelancers to keep fixed cost low. It does not have any external investors, but the founders plan to apply for VC in the future. It received government support amounting to 30,000 MXN, equivalent to about 1,400 EUR (European Central Bank, 2019). Start-up C completed two programs with TecLean, including Tec Launchpad which is currently called TecLean Growth. Start-up C is not formally part of any incubation program but uses the services like mentoring and the office space in return for sharing their expertise with new start-ups in biotech. The interview was conducted with the CTO. Several elements of Start-up C's MCS were implemented by its initiative and without the incubator's help. A formal weekly meeting and a Gantt diagram for quarterly meetings have been established. The implementation was driven by one of the co-founder's studies and experience in industrial engineering and project management. Start-up C has implemented a sales forecast to understand when to invest in growing its business and due to a previously experienced shortage of its product. Start-up C has implemented Performance Targets to control its margins, to compare the performance between months and to facilitate the planning process. While the incubator does not require a dress code, Start-up C has implemented this due to their direct work with clients. A cash budget was introduced because of high operating expenses (OPEX). The CTO explains: "It's that our OPEX, our operation expenses, somehow were too high, so we assign like a percentage of the total income to the OPEX to keep it under control, this one was real experience." Start-up C uses the online-tool "Trello" as a checklist and dashboard. This has been introduced since the co-founders were doing redundant work; TecLean had aided in the implementation. The CTO states: "Most of the people make the job twice. So that's why we have to create the dashboard. It's Trello, it's free online and a lot of the entrepreneurs here use it. So basically they [TecLean] told us how to make the checklist." Two systems were implemented due to encouragement from TecLean, but without TecLean's help, since the incubator focuses on start-ups in the Information Technology (IT) sector. The co-founders started to measure ROI after making it their main business aiming at controlling their investments and expected returns. Similarly, Start-up C uses a Variance Analysis after TecLean's advice. The CTO explains: "[The Variance Analysis] was more [related] to the incubator, they encourage you to for instance do Data Analysis and ours is more simple, but yeah, they encouraged us to do it, but how to do it has to be more from experience." Lastly, Start-up C uses several systems that TecLean advised to implement and support in the implementation. It has a formal organizational structure between the three co-founders, dividing the positions into chief operating officer (COO), CEO and CTO. TecLean consulted Start-up C on how to manage the share allocation and the formal constitution of the start-up. Start-up C gives rewards in the form of bonuses or good reviews for freelancers who finished their project on time. Statements of mission and vision were implemented, as well as their massive transformative purpose: "Creating wellness with biotech." The CTO argues: "We have to have a One Pager, basically have a description of what you do, having your mission, your vision and your mantra." Start-up C's initiative to implement certain systems was often experience based and related to its mentors' advice. The CTO also describes that the start-up needs to systematize many processes for being able to apply for VC. While Start-up C participated in TecLean to formalize, the implementation of their systems often had to be based on their own experience due to TecLean's focus on IT. TecLean encouraged Start-up C to keep the systems simple. Peer pressure was also a factor impacting the systems implemented. The CTO describes: "Well, basically, the incubator helped us formalize a lot of things, like, we were formal; let's say formal in the beginning, but let's say that the incubator told us how the things are done corporate; they taught us how to make your enterprise look great so that people can trust you or an investor can trust you. The incubator basically teaches you how to keep the systems simple. And it's like peer-pressure, being with many other entrepreneurs, you start doing the same stuff".

Cross-Case Analysis

While management and entrepreneurs agree that an incubation process in the growth phase of a start-up is not standardized but rather problem based, the key offerings for start-ups seem to be the co-working space, workshops, networking and mentoring. Most fundamentally, the start-ups make use of mentoring from people inside and outside the incubator. The incubator's management explains that they do not specifically aim at providing advice in management accounting but focus on business models, investments and basic legal matters. The start-ups implemented their MCS gradually by adding new mechanisms, systems and routines. It can be observed that the start-ups initiated the implementation of several mechanisms and systems themselves; either reactively due to previously experienced problems or proactively due to the managers' professional background and knowledge. Their implementation was either fully autonomous or supported by TecLean's mentors. A pattern emerges when looking at the systems that TecLean proposed to implement. In two of the start-ups, TecLean specifically suggested the creation of a variance analysis, potentially for being able to monitor the start-ups' progress themselves. Interestingly, many of the systems proposed by TecLean focused explicitly on external stakeholders. In two of the start-ups, freelancers are not a supplement but a substitute for employees due to legal reasons or to keep fixed costs low. Therefore, TecLean suggested systems specifically aiming at controlling freelancers' behavior. Examples include bonuses for salespeople, checklists for freelancing artists, specific contracts for freelancers, legal courses and other benefits. In Start-up A's case TecLean advised to implement external performance targets specifically for clients and supported the design of these targets. While all three start-ups mentioned that TecLean, in general, encouraged them to formalize, Start-up A's director emphasizes several times that TecLean taught them to keep the systems simple to facilitate growth. In all three cases, TecLean pushes the implementation of MCSs beyond the traditional conceptualizations as being "formal" and beyond organizational borders to align stakeholders' interests with the start-ups' goals. Additionally, the start-ups introduced many software-related systems that they had observed from other entrepreneurs in the incubator, including the Task Management software *Coophi* and *Trello*. It appears that start-ups are able to imitate the best practices from their peers. Simultaneously, Start-up C's CTO mentions peer pressure as an additional factor. He describes that start-ups that operate in a similar context adjust to common practices within that environment.

Finally, by advising start-ups on how to do things in a "corporate" manner, TecLean aims at increasing the start-ups' credibility toward potential future investors. The two start-ups, A and C, that had concrete plans to apply for VC had significantly more elements and systems within their MCS and can be described as being more formal. Figure 1 summarizes the factors impacting the start-ups' MCSs and their interrelation.

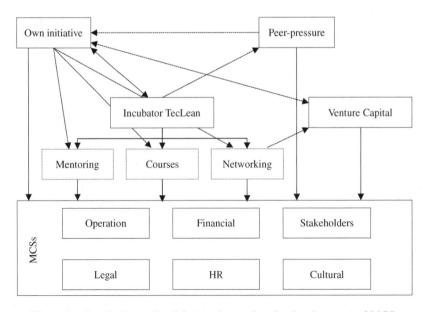

Figure 1.   Incubation-related factors impacting the development of MCSs

Discussion

This research aims to explore how an incubation process may impact the MCSs in start-ups. First, this research aligns with previous findings from Davila *et al.* (2010) that internal factors are one primary driver in the adoption of MCSs in start-ups; even when the start-ups are part of an incubation process. Specifically, two factors identified by Davila *et al.* (2010) are reflected in this research. Previously experienced problems, such as product shortage, encouraged the entrepreneurs to adopt more formal systems or routines. Besides, the entrepreneurs' academic background also led to the implementation of specific systems or routines. While studies have acknowledged external factors in the adoption of MCSs, they have not previously considered to include BIs. The findings of this research suggest that an incubation process is a further relevant external factor impacting the development of MCSs in start-ups. This research finds evidence that the incubation process pushes the start-ups toward a non-traditional conceptualization of MCSs. The BI's advice in legal and strategic matters is a decisive factor in a start-up's choice of legal form and business model. Consequences include the substitution of employees with freelancers for legal or operational reasons. The BI then assists the start-ups in shifting the focus of their MCSs from employees to external stakeholders, such as freelancers or even clients. This finding contrasts directly with the previously applied definition of MCSs from Merchant and van der Stede (2017) or Collins (1982). They argue that MCSs are designed to control employees within an organization. Other definitions focus on factors inside of an organization (Simons, 1995) or very broadly on goal achievement (Cunningham, 1992). This research, however, indicates that MCSs in start-ups may be directed explicitly toward their stakeholders. This extends the knowledge of previous research by Malmi and Brown (2008) who argue that it could be relevant to investigate the stakeholder's perspective in Performance Measurement elements of MCSs. This research adds that the stakeholders' perspective is not only relevant in Performance Measurement, but in the design of MCSs as a whole. This stakeholder perspective has been widely neglected in literature, especially when studying start-ups.

Lastly, another external factor impacting the development of MCSs in start-ups is commonly argued to be the presence of VC (Davila, 2000; Davila *et al.*, 2010, 2015; Granlund & Taipaleenmäki, 2005). In the investigated start-ups, neither was VC not present nor did the start-ups mention to be in negotiations with potential investors. Nevertheless, it appears that the concrete plan to apply for VC increases the number and formality of systems implemented within an MCS. This was driven by the start-ups' participation in the BI. The incubation process taught start-ups how to create credibility toward investors by formalizing their systems. Entrepreneurs were familiar with the need to formalize not only to grow their business but to obtain investment. This finding extends the study of Davila *et al.* (2015), who argue that start-ups with more formal systems commonly achieve a higher company valuation. This research indicates that entrepreneurs are aware of an MCS's value for investors and are thus consciously implementing MCSs before applying to VC.

Conclusion

This research concludes that a BI may impact the development of MCSs in start-ups mainly in two ways. First, it pushes the start-ups toward a non-traditional conceptualization of MCSs beyond organizational borders, focusing specifically on stakeholders such as freelancers and clients. Following Alvesson and Sandberg (2011), this is a highly relevant finding by problematizing the current definition of MCSs in start-ups. This research contributes to management accounting and entrepreneurship literature by suggesting to include the stakeholders' perspective in the definition of MCSs for start-ups. Second, this research adds to the existing literature by arguing that a BI may teach a start-up how to create credibility toward external investors. A BI can thus increase the awareness and initiative of entrepreneurs to implement stronger MCSs even before applying to VC. The findings of this research are relevant in practice. They suggest that so far, incubation processes do not intentionally make it their goal to create strong MCSs in start-ups. By consciously choosing to teach entrepreneurs in the design of MCSs and by highlighting MCSs' benefits, BIs may increase the survival rates of the incubated start-ups and VC may become more accessible for them.

This research has two main limitations. First, while measures have been taken to prevent the response bias, it is not possible to entirely eliminate this in qualitative research. Only one person per start-up was available for interviews and start-ups did not follow the request to share internal documents with the researcher. Future research might benefit from taking different approaches for data triangulation by including field observations and internal documents in the data collection. Second, regarding the operationalization of MCSs, it needs to be acknowledged that this research does not measure how good the implemented MCSs are. It does not measure the effect that MCSs have on the performance or valuation of an organization, but it investigates the reason for the implementation of MCSs and the intention with which they were designed. Future research could focus on operationalizing the quality of MCSs and investigate whether an incubation process is an influencing factor in the quality of MCSs.

References

Ahrens, T. & Chapman, C.S. (2006). Doing qualitative field research in management accounting: positioning data to contribute to theory. *Accounting, Organizations and Society*, 31(8), 819–841.

Alvesson, M. & Sandberg, J. (2011). Generating research questions through problematization. *Academy of Management Review*, 36(2), 247–271.

Autio, E., Nambisan, S., Thomas, L.D.W. & Wright, M. (2018). Digital affordances, spatial affordances, and the genesis of entrepreneurial ecosystems. *Strategic Entrepreneurship Journal*, 12(1), 72–95.

Bergek, A. & Norrman, C. (2008). Incubator best practice: A framework. *Technovation*, 28(1), 20–28.

Bruneel, J., Ratinho, T., Clarysse, B. & Groen, A. (2012). The evolution of business incubators: comparing demand and supply of business incubation services across different incubator generations. *Technovation*, 32(2), 110–121.

Bryman, A. & Bell, E. (2007). *Business Research Methods*, 2nd Edn. Oxford: Oxford University Press.

Collins, F. (1982). Managerial accounting systems and organizational control: A role perspective. Accounting, Organizations and Society, 7(2), 107–122.

Coyte, R. (2019). Enabling management control systems, situated learning and intellectual capital development. *Accounting, Auditing & Accountability Journal*, 32(4), 1073–1097.

Cunningham, G.M. (1992). Management control and accounting systems under a competitive strategy. *Accounting, Auditing & Accountability Journal*, 5(2), 85–102.

Davila, A. (2000). An empirical study on the drivers of management control systems' design in new product development. *Accounting, Organizations and Society*, 25(4), 383–409.

Davila, A. & Foster, G. (2007). Management control systems in early-stage startup companies. *The Accounting Review*, 82(4), 907–937.

Davila, A., Foster, G. & Jia, N. (2010). Building sustainable high-growth startup companies: management systems as an accelerator. *California Management Review*, 52(3), 79–105.

Davila, A., Foster, G. & Jia, N. (2015). The valuation of management control systems in start-up companies: international field-based evidence. *European Accounting Review*, 24(2), 207–239.

Diefenbach, U., Wald, A. & Gleich, R. (2018). Between cost and benefit: investigating effects of cost management control systems on cost efficiency and organizational performance. *Journal of Management Control*, 29(1), 63–89.

Eisenhardt, K.M. (1989). Building theories from case study research. *Academy of Management Review*, 14(4), 532–550.

European Central Bank (2019). ECB euro reference exchange rate: Mexican peso (MXN). Retrieved from: https://www.ecb.europa.eu/stats/policy_and_exchange_rates/euro_reference_exchange_rates/html/eurofxref-graph-mxn.en.html [Accessed on September 10, 2019].

Freeman, J. & Engel, J.S. (2007). Models of innovation: startups and mature corporations. *California Management Review*, 50(1), 94–119.

Granlund, M. & Taipaleenmäki, J. (2005). Management control and controllership in new economy firms—a life cycle perspective. *Management Accounting Research*, 16(1), 21–57.

Hackett, S.M. & Dilts, D.M. (2004). A systematic review of business incubation research. *Journal of Technology Transfer*, 29(1), 55–82.

Junqueira, E., Dutra, E.V., Zanquetto Filho, H. & Gonzaga, R.P. (2016). The effect of strategic choices and management control systems on organizational performance. Revista *Contabilidade & Finanças*, 27(72), 334–348.

Knight, K.E. (1967). A descriptive model of the intra-firm innovation process. *The Journal of Business*, 40(4), 478–496.

Lee, B. & Humphrey, C. (2006). More than a numbers game: qualitative research in accounting. *Management Decision*, 44(2), 180–197.

Lowe, E.A. (1971). On the idea of a management control system: Integrating accounting and management control. *Journal of Management Studies*, 8(1), 1–12.

Lukka, K. & Modell, S. (2010). Validation in interpretive management accounting research. *Accounting, Organizations and Society*, 35(4), 462–477.

Malmi, T. & Brown, D.A. (2008). Management control systems as a package—Opportunities, challenges and research directions. *Management Accounting Research*, 19(4), 287–300.

Merchant, K. & van der Stede, W.A. (2017). Management control systems: Performance measurement. In: *Evaluation and Incentives*, 4th Edn. Harlow: Pearson.

Mian, S., Lamine, W. & Fayolle, A. (2016). Technology business incubation: An overview of the state of knowledge. *Technovation*, 50–51, 1–12.

Miller, D. & Friesen, P.H. (1984). A longitudinal study of the corporate life cycle. *Management Science*, 30(10), 1161–1183.

Pierce, J.L. & Delbecq, A.L. (1977). Organization structure, individual attitudes and innovation. *The Academy of Management Review*, 2(1), 27–37.

Quinlan, C., Babin, B.J., Carr, J., Griffin, M. & Zikmund, W.G. (2015). *Business Research Methods*. Hampshire: Cengage Learning EMEA.

Rubin, T.H., Aas, T.H. & Stead, A. (2015). Knowledge flow in technological business incubators: Evidence from Australia and Israel. *Technovation*, 41–42, 11–24.

Samagaio, A., Crespo, N.F. & Rodrigues, R. (2018). Management control systems in high-tech start-ups: An empirical investigation. *Journal of Business Research*, 89, 351–360.

Saunders, M., Lewis, P. & Thornhill, A. (2016). *Research Methods for Business Students*, 7th Edn. Harlow: Pearson.

Scapens, R.W. (2004). Doing case study research. In: C. Humphrey (ed.), *The Real Life Guide to Accounting Research: A Behind-The-Scenes View of Using Qualitative Research Methods*. Amsterdam: Elsevier, pp. 257–279.

Schramm, C.J. (2004). Building entrepreneurial economies. *Foreign Affairs*, 83(4), 104–115.

Simons, R. (1995). *Levers of Control: How Managers Use Innovative Control Systems to Drive Strategic Renewal*. Boston, Massachusetts: Harvard Business School Press.

Strauss, E.R., Nevries, P. & Weber, J. (2013). The development of MCS packages – balancing constituents' demands. *Journal of Accounting & Organizational Change*, 9(2), 155–187.

Todd, J. (1977). Research: management control systems: A key link between strategy a structure and employee performance. *Organizational Dynamics*, 5(4), 65–78.

Torres-Preciado, V.H., Polanco-Gaytán, M. & Tinoco-Zermeño, M.Á. (2014). Technological innovation and regional economic growth in Mexico: a spatial perspective. *The Annals of Regional Science*, 52(1), 183–200.

Yin, R.K. (2018). *Case Study Research and Applications: Design and Methods*, 6th Edn. Thousand Oaks, California: Sage.

Chapter 9

Toward a Better Understanding of the ICTs' Role in the Creation of Social Networks

Sihem Ben Saad[*,‡] and Fatma Choura[†,§]

*Carthage Business School, University of Tunis Carthage,
Tunis, Tunisia*

†*Higher Institute of Computer Science, Tunis El Manar University,
Tunis, Tunisia*
‡*sihem.bensaad87@gmail.com*
§*fatma.choura@isi.utm.tn*

This chapter seeks to identify the information and communication technologies (ICTs) that may amplify the user's communication process within the context of an emerging market. To better understand the importance of ICTs and the users' psychological states against these devices, we base our theoretical framework on the theory of social response. A qualitative analysis was conducted to better understand the role of ICTs in the creation of social networks. Our results allow for the identification of virtual anthropomorphic agents and commercial discussion forums with specific characteristics as main technologies that can enhance the presence experience on a commercial site. They can also offer virtual atmosphere, allowing the creation of social links. These technologies may influence the user's psychological states (i.e. state of flow and telepresence experience) as well as his approach behavior. It is therefore essential for designers of commercial websites to put forward sophisticated ICTs. Thanks to these tools, it is now possible to offer content that is valued on the sensory level for Internet users. Consequently, commercial websites should move from a utilitarian dimension to a hedonistic one.

Introduction

The transfer of technologies to emerging countries is a phenomenon that could lead to economic progress for companies operating online. Indeed, the emerging countries are experiencing major advances in the technological field: they appropriate the latest technologies and exploit their benefits. Nowadays, information and communication technologies (ICTs) have the special character of generic technologies of value. The purpose of this study is to identify the types of ICTs that can boost the user's communication process within the context of an emerging market. Virtually all emerging countries are engaged in a process of exploring/exploiting the opportunities offered by ICTs (Groth *et al.*, 2019). The emergence of ICTs offers emerging markets a wide range of generic technologies for better use of information, opportunities to reduce transaction and coordination costs, opportunities to exploit new markets as well as opportunities to enhance the content of their products and services. For this purpose, the new technologies have witnessed a widespread implementation and a huge overgeneralization in emerging economies. ICTs are recognized as key elements of a company's development by carrying out its activity online. They are also considered a source of innovation and knowledge creation. Indeed, ICTs are emerging as a new mode of interactive communication, aiming to improve information management between the Internet users and the online company. Internet is nowadays a requisite tool for companies' activities that makes its role as a marketing channel indisputable. Several researchers stated that despite the important role of web as online marketing channel, there are still many unanswered questions regarding the optimization of these sites' interactivity to ensure a sustainable competitive advantage (Charfi & Volle, 2010; Groth *et al.*, 2019; Van Doorn *et al.*, 2017). Groth *et al.* (2019) found that the creation of an attractive and a custom-made environment are conditional on the development of the presence experience in a commercial website. The choice of relevant theatrical technologies used to influence visitors' perception and re-enchant them and the problem of differentiation deserve a deeper investigation. Those technologies are based on interactions between the user and the merchant environment. Moreover, the extant literature on the themes of the commercial Web sites' interactivity suggests that the technical dimension that refers to the elements of a virtual purchasing environment is able to stimulate the sense and affect the user's perceptual field (Charfi & Volle, 2010). Nevertheless, it does not produce the fiction that the user is interacting with another person and not with a machine. In fact, an imbalance is recorded in the literature regarding the two interactivity dimensions where the technical dimension continues to be the subject of more researches than the social one. The potential effects of the latter dimension on the user's behavior are key motivations to carry out this study. To meet this need, our research has three objectives. The first objective consists of identifying the main ICTs with strong emotional potential. The second objective is to highlight the psychological states felt by the user with regard to these technologies. The final goal is to explore the prospective behavioral consequences of these devices. The remainder of this chapter is organized as follows. The next section discusses the theoretical framework of the theory of social response and debates the social dimension of interactivity, the communication through ICTs and the psychological state felt by the user. The penultimate section develops the methodological details about the empirical process, sample and tools used to collect the requested information. The last section presents the main results of this study. We conclude the chapter by a discussion of the findings, implications and new perspectives of research.

Literature Review and Hypotheses

To better understand the importance of ICTs as well as the psychological states of users against these devices, this study retains the theory of social response as the main theoretical framework.

Theory of Social Response

The theory of social response assumes that users are able to interact with computers as well as with social actors and that they use among each other social responses usually reserved for interactions between humans (Lemoine & Cherif, 2015; Nass *et al.*, 1995). Social response theory assumes that Internet users can interact with their computers as well as with humans (Lemoine & Cherif, 2015; Nass *et al.*, 1995;

Steuer & Nass, 1993). Language, voice, interactivity and social role are the different variables that can reinforce the social aspect of an online experience. In terms of language and voice, because computers use human language and voice, users behave as if they are facing different people (Steuer & Nass, 1993; Turkle, 1984; Bressoles *et al.*, 2014). As for interactivity, Wang *et al.* (2007) consider that when the interaction with a merchant website is similar to human and interpersonal interactions, users behave as if they were facing a real physical person. Finally, actual study finds that the social role is attributed to the site. To facilitate the navigation of the user, it is possible to use as an example a virtual agent. To reproduce the feeling of a social presence online, marketing managers use certain means such as virtual anthropomorphic agents. Interactivity is a very old concept that has evolved along with the evolution of technology. The literature distinguishes two aspects of interactivity: (1) the technical aspect as it relates to design factors such as color, music, quality of electronic services, design and ease of use (Steuer, 1992; Mollen & Wilson, 2010); and (2) the social features which refer to social factors often related to the notion of interpersonal human interaction (Huang & Lin, 2007; Almeida *et al.*, 2014; Ben Saad & Choura, 2016; Blazevis *et al.*, 2014; Garramone & Anderson, 1986; Groth *et al.*, 2019).

Social Interactivity: A Distinctive Element in a Commercial Site

Literature review revealed the importance of the presence of virtual reality devices in e-commerce (Bush *et al.*, 2014; Ben Saad & Choura, 2016; Garramone & Anderson, 1986; Van Doorn *et al.*, 2017). Some researchers underlined that these tools must be incorporated into a virtual merchant site to stimulate visitors' positive emotions (Cyr *et al.*, 2007; Gensler *et al.*, 2013; Lemoine, 2012; Van Doorn *et al.*, 2017), while others highlight the perception of a warm and sociable site (Garramone & Anderson, 1986; Sandelands & Buckner, 1989; Bathelt & Turi, 2011; Allen *et al.*, 2014). Equally, additional investigations showed that Internet users are increasingly looking for social interactions (Disbach *et al.*, 2007; Thrau *et al.*, 2013; Blazevis *et al.*, 2014). The presence of a virtual agent or commercial discussion forums is able to respond to the consumer's complaints and develop the user's sense of human interaction (Bressoles & Viot, 2014; Bressoles *et al.*, 2014; Lemoine, 2012; Thrau *et al.*, 2013).

In particular, the presence of an anthropomorphic virtual agent, with interactive human characteristics corresponds to a stronger perception of interactivity (Steuer, 1992; Lemoine, 2012). In fact, virtual agents are designed to help Internet users navigate commercial websites. They can guide the consumers to new products and help the users during their navigations. They can also improve the quality of the exchanges between the company and the consumer and develop the interactivity of virtual merchant environments to ease the access to knowledge.

The role of virtual agents has been demonstrated in the fields of the consumers' relations and communication of online companies. Previous investigations put into evidence how the sense of social presence can be reinforced by some technologies that facilitates interpersonal communication and personalizes the communication exchanges (Evrard *et al.*, 2009; Ben Saad & Choura, 2016). Furthermore, other researchers argued that the success of commercial sites depends on their ability to generate the state of flow and to allow the user to experience the telepresence experience in a virtual environment (Groth *et al.*, 2019; Hoffman & Novak, 2009).

Communication through ICTs: A Strategic Innovative Source

Communication via ICTs has become an essential informational vector between the online company and the consumer. ICTs aim to improve and facilitate data circulation. Communication through ICTs must be regular and accessible. For this purpose, virtual anthropomorphic agents and commercial discussion forums are considered as assistants to ease the traffic knowledge and information sharing. On this basis, interactivity is a key management variable in virtual market environments.

In this research, the state of flow and the experience of telepresence are identified as potential consequences of the virtual agent's anthropomorphism and commercial discussion forum (Blazevis *et al.*, 2014; Ben Saad and Choura, 2017; Jauréguibéry and Proulx, 2017; Zahao *et al.*, 2015). These two variables are crucial for the description of human–machine interactions.

The State of Flow and the Experience of Telepresence in Online Experiential Contexts

First introduced by Csikszentmihalyi (1990), the concept of "state of flow" refers to a state lived by highly involved Internet users in a given activity. A feeling of control, a perception of challenge and a feeling of being physically present in a mediated environment determine this state. The state of flow is thus a fundamental element in the characterization of human–machine interactions. Some researchers valued the utility of creating the "telepresence experience" to describe the interactions in a mediated environment (Lemoine, 2012). This concept illustrates how the user develops a feeling of being physically present in a virtual environment.

Toward a Conceptualization of the Impact of ICTs: A Qualitative Study

Social interactivity is currently emerging as a virtual reality device with persuasive powers and growing importance for market web designers and e-commerce professionals. Within this framework, the purpose of this study is to identify the main ICTs that may amplify the user's communication and imagination process and to tackle their possible effects on psychological states and behavioral responses. More specifically, we aim to explore the Tunisian context through a qualitative approach and detect the importance of interactivity in commercial sites through the reactions that it can generate and the competitive advantage that it can grant to the company.

Methodology

The exploratory approach was favored to foster a better understanding of the perception and persuasive powers of interactivity. Such approach allows us to discern the main psychological states felt by the user during his visits on websites containing interactive tools. Semi-structured individual interviews were conducted with 82 respondents; all of them had previously visited a merchant website. The participants are adults aged between 22 and 66 years and have different socio-professional profiles (students, teachers, managers, etc.). It is a sample of convenience with a huge diversity of profiles in terms of socio-demographic characteristics. However, the required satisfactory level of familiarity with the Internet tools and online purchase was achieved. The average duration of an interview was about 40 min (see Table 1).

Table 1.   Composition of respondents' sample (*n* = 82)

Characteristics of the respondents	Percentage
Gender	
Male	50
Female	50
Age Interval	
22–34 years	75
35–66 years	25
Frequency of Internet Use	
Several times per day	47
Several times per week	35
Several times per month	18
Frequency of Online Purchase	
Once per month	85
Several times per month	15

An experimental website was designed the content of which dealt with online sales of fashion clothes for men, women and babies. Several pages provided information on various offers, payment methods, etc. (Appendix 1). In addition, it includes some virtual reality devices, such as the presence of an anthropomorphic virtual agent and a commercial discussion forum. As a first step, each interviewee was invited to visit our experimental website. The online visit was planned in a quiet location fitted with computers and a high-speed Internet connection. The use of in-depth individual interviews facilitated the collection of rich, detailed information based on the interviewee's experience (Evrard *et al.*, 2009). The construction of the interview guide was based on the funnel technique to get a smooth transition from the general to the specific themes to best meet the purpose of the study: (1) Identification of the focal elements of the website that caught the user's attention; (2) Detection of the typical features of the virtual environments; (3) Understanding of the psychological states of Internet users while visiting interactive commercial websites; and (4) Understanding of the behavioral intentions of visitor's merchant websites. Equally, to take into account the semantic saturation, the content analysis was carried out simultaneously with the data collection (Evrard *et al.*, 2009).

Results

The content analysis employed in all the interviews decrypted the four main themes presented previously.

In what follows, we present the results of the thematic content analysis that we performed. The method is based on cutting of the whole content according to the criterion of meaning and then regrouping them verbatim into homogeneous themes: *Definition and perception of interactivity by the participants.* Respondents reported that the elements that caught their attention were related to the ergonomics of the website and atmospheric variables — *colors, ease of use, animation of images and sounds.* This supports the study by Mollen and Wilson (2010), who stated that interactivity could be defined according to its technical dimension, and the *Distinctive Experiential Components of Media Environments with High Emotional Potential.* To sort out a meaningful representation of the experiential components, we applied the typology of Baker (1986). This typology presents a classification of environmental attributes into three categories: environmental, design and social factors. The verbatim allowed us to extract two main components, namely the anthropomorphic characteristics of the virtual agent and the characteristics of the commercial discussion group (group involvement, receptivity and similarity).

The Anthropomorphic Characteristics of the Virtual Agent

The analysis of qualitative materials highlighted the attention to virtual anthropomorphic agents. Respondents confirmed that commercial websites are dehumanized (there is no interactive website in Tunisia; I want an interactive website that has a virtual agent capable of expressing emotions). The analysis revealed that the interaction with a virtual anthropomorphic agent could be similar to an interpersonal exchange and allowed for rich exchanges. Moreover, the website's visitors had reacted to the computer as if they were facing a real physical person (to have an agent that directs you to the website with customized and specific needs answers, talking to a specialized salesperson who has the ability to speak, to move behind his computer). These statements refer to the definition set by several studies indicating that virtual agents could take many forms and play various roles (Blazevis *et al.*, 2014; Charfi, 2012; Cook, 1994; Csikszentmihalyi, 1990). Among the experiential components, the anthropomorphism of the virtual agent was the first one to be mentioned. This type of virtual agent has the ability to act, react, talk and move. His behavior may vary over time. It is characterized by the extent of its features. Seeking to maximize the sense of social presence in virtual shopping environments, the respondents are increasingly concerned not only about the usefulness of the virtual agent's presence but also about his ritual behavior (Groth *et al.*, 2019). In fact, the presence of a simple virtual agent with only conversational abilities is no longer enough and it is essential to consider their ritual behavior while interacting with the user.

The Characteristics of the Commercial Discussion Group

Interviewees focused on the importance of discussion forums' presence in commercial websites "Personally I want to chat with other visitors to help me in my choices, I want a space in the website to put my comments." This supported the conclusions of previous research pointing out that Internet users are increasingly looking for social interaction (Ben Saad & Choura, 2013; Bressoles *et al.*, 2014; Sandelands & Buckner, 1989). To cope with these user's preferences, many companies have included discussion forums on their websites (Disbach *et al.*, 2007). The verbatim also revealed that some interviewees attempted to appropriate the virtual space by seeking to explore specific characteristics of the commercial focus group, such as the receptivity of the group and its involvement. (The group must be receptive to our opinions, it must answer our questions; the discussion group must be open to my ideas.) Theme 3 involves the psychological states felt by the user against an interactive media environment. The two experimental components of the virtual environment contributed to positive states for the user. The analysis of the interview's results revealed that the state of flow is the sentiment felt by the users when they visit an interactive commercial website. In fact, they can express a feeling of playfulness and total immersion. In addition, they express a feeling of total concentration that would correspond to an extraordinary experience (I feel a warmer welcome leading to the advertiser's willingness to meet the consumer's expectations; a sense of playfulness, more at ease, I feel a great pleasure), (I was curious, I was waiting for the rest, I appreciated, I found it original, I was always concentrated and focused. We are directly told what makes us more focused; I think it is a success, I visited the Renault's French website; frankly it was a pleasant visit that involved me throughout my navigation).

The above outputs are consistent with the results of Lorna *et al.* (2019), who argued that to successfully live a state of flow during his online shopping, the user needs to be intensively playful, fully focused, perfectly in control of his navigation and truly in confrontation with challenges. A feeling of telepresence in an interactive environment was also mentioned in the corpus. In fact, the respondents described that they experienced moments of strong emotions and felt like they were in a real virtual world (I have the feeling that I am physically existent in this environment that seemed real to me; it's like I'm in front of a real agent, physical; I am intensively absorbed when I visit a commercial website containing an animated agent, it attempts me, I forget everything that exists around me). Similarly, the results of Lemoine and Notebaert (2011) revealed that the telepresence experience is the psychological state of being present in a computer-mediated environment, augmented by a focused attention. The state of flow and the experience of telepresence can play a mediating role in the relationship between the social interactivity and the user's behavioral approach. Indeed, Gensler *et al.* (2013) show that, in computer-mediated environments, the state of flow and the telepresence experience are central concepts in the explanation of the psychological states felt by the user and his behavioral approach in the media environments. We also found that the user has a risk perception during his shopping in a virtual environment. Some interviewees expressed a sense of perceived risk to virtual environments (I would be frankly afraid to buy virtually, I would be doubtful to receive the same product that I ordered, I feel unable to judge the quality of a product, it's complicated to choose a product in the Internet). Theme 4 deals with behavioral intentions on interactive websites. Virtual environments are designed to create positive effects for Internet users, both cognitively and emotionally (Gensler *et al.*, 2013). However, Groth *et al.* (2019) pointed out "consumer experience includes activities that will influence the decisions and future actions of consumers." In fact, some experimental elements, such as the anthropomorphism of the virtual agent and the characteristics of the commercial discussion group, can lead to behavioral changes. For example, under certain conditions, the presence of sophisticated virtual agents can improve the user's exploratory behavior and his online presence time (Ben Saad & Choura, 2016; Pelet *et al.*, 2014).

Interviewees identified that an interactive commercial website has a positive impact on the user's behavioral approach (An interactive website containing, for example a virtual agent reflects the website, so it will encourage users to buy by giving them the information they want; the likelihood that I choose the same website for my next purchase is very high. Others say that an interactive website can generate positive word of mouth on the Internet (I will recommend this website to all my friends and anyone who asks me for advice; I spoke favorably of this website). Furthermore, our thematic analysis displayed that virtual reality devices have a significant impact on the phenomenon of electronic word of mouth and the user's behavioral approach.

Synthesis and Discussion of the Results

The primary goal of this research is to identify the ICTs that may amplify the user's communication process within the context of an emerging market. Such ICTs are now considered a requisite in the demands of Internet users. Indeed, the participants in our study expressed strong attachment not only to the presence of a simple virtual agent but also to its anthropomorphism. This type of agent is incarnated; it has cognitive, biological and emotional dimensions that the literature synthesizes in anthropomorphism of the virtual agent. The closer the agent to human behavior, the less the website is perceived cold, distant and impersonal. The more anthropomorphic characteristics are attributed to the virtual agent, the more this device humanizes the human–machine interface and the more the website is perceived warm and sociable. On the contrary, the commercial discussion forum is equally considered as a new virtual reality device that has gained the attention of many researchers (Garramone *et al.*, 2013; Hoffman & Novak, 2009; Sandelands & Buckner, 1989), who stressed out that Internet users are increasingly in need of social interaction, in addition to their instrumental goals. However, as part of this work, Internet users are more and more concerned about the characteristics of commercial discussion forums, such as group involvement, similarity and receptivity. In fact, the more the forum is engaged in interaction, the more this technology enriches the user's visit, the more members of the group listen to others' ideas and the more the presence of this device makes it possible to improve the online company's performance. The relation between social interactivity and the user's behavioral approach can include a set of variables that may play a mediating role, such as the state of flow, the experience of telepresence and the phenomenon of electronic word of mouth. Based on these observations, virtual reality devices have a fundamental function in e-commerce websites. They activate the user's psychological states, such as his state of flow and experience of telepresence. In addition, within this conceptual framework, it seems appropriate to retain the perceived risk from the qualitative study. Lemoine and Notebaert (2011) argued that the risk felt by Internet users of this mode of marketing to order their desired products has increased. In fact, the perceived risk refers to the feeling of anxiety that a user can experience in a mediated environment. It can counterbalance the feeling of playfulness, being present in a virtual environment and even the user's behavior.

The Theoretical Contributions of the Research

While many studies on interactivity have examined the impact of its technical dimension on trust, the intention to buy and the satisfaction of users (e.g. Mollen & Wilson, 2010), the main interest of this research is to sensitize the marketing researchers on the importance of ICTs. Our investigations reveal that two original devices seem to have an impact on the merchant websites: (1) The first relates mainly to the anthropomorphic characteristics of the virtual agent. Particularly, this refers to the artificial intelligence of virtual agents. These agents are defined by many researchers as animated characters with a certain capacity for ritual behavior. In fact, numerous studies on virtual agents have reported a positive impact of their presence on the performance of online companies (Charfi, 2012; Groth *et al.*, 2019; Lemoine, 2012; Takahashi *et al.*, 2000). More precisely, we believe that it is rather crucial to deepen the analysis on the anthropomorphic characteristics of the virtual agent, the psychological states of the user (flow status and telepresence experience) and on efficiency variables such as behavioral approach. (2) The second original device refers to the characteristics of the commercial discussion group. To develop the behavioral approach that Internet users experienced with commercial websites is a necessity. This new device enables to humanize the human–machine interface and to develop the sense of belonging among users. Does setting up a discussion space in a merchant website make it possible to extend the user's visit time and optimize the feeling of social presence on the website? Certainly, this technology would strengthen the social bond. Through this research, we wanted to pave the way for multiple studies to test the characteristics of commercial discussion forums (such as group involvement, receptivity and similarity) on the user's behavioral approach.

Experiments on the user's affective reactions contributed to the field of research on the state of flow and the experience of telepresence, which remains a vast field to investigate. From a theoretical point of view, the main contribution of this research is to propose a conceptualization of the experimental components of the website with strong emotional potential. Like physical outlets, these components provoked emotional reactions among Internet users to the feelings of playfulness and being physically present in a media environment. This study makes several contributions to the existing literature on different innovation technologies. Various classifications have been developed to classify the different forms of interactive functionality that can be integrated into a digital medium. Thus, our study makes an important input in revealing the need to subdivide the social dimension of interactivity into two aspects, namely those related to external and internal communications. This distinction is based on the fact that some innovation technologies facilitate human interaction between the user and the website through the presence of a virtual anthropomorphic agent, while others make easy the human interactions between Internet users and the commercial discussion forums with interactive features. In the context of virtual environments, our results demonstrate that different external and internal communication technologies have the same effect on how a consumer experiences digital media. More specifically, both types of technology increase the sense of social presence, the state of flow and the feeling of being physically present in a remote environment.

The Managerial Contributions of the Research

The managerial contributions of our findings consist in suggesting tools that would be able to enhance the online shopping experience. Companies are increasingly looking for commercial websites design that can attract, retain and convince Internet users. This study identifies the elements that contribute the most to a potential pleasant experience and experimental components that are important to invest in. If the majority of commercial websites fall short of sensory stimuli, our study highlights the anthropo-morphism of the virtual agent and focuses on the characteristics of the commercial focus group. These devices can improve the performance of a web-based business. They present endless possibilities for marketing professionals, especially in terms of creating an interactive experience for Internet users. Our results show that the social dimensions of interactivity are key elements for online brands. Virtual reality devices influence the emotional state of Internet users. As a result, the designers of the market interfaces have to give more importance to the creation of original online experience, because when Internet competition is at its peak, the utility function is no longer the one that differentiates virtual environments from one another, but the hedonic function that is a key success factor (Charfi, 2012).

Limits and Future Perspectives of the Research

The results of this study demonstrate the importance of integrating ICTs to promote the internal and external communication of online companies. These ICTs have the ability to positively affect the consumer's psycho-logical responses. If one of these technologies disappears, the psycho-logical states of the consumer would be positively influenced by the other technology. Thus, they highlight the feeling of belonging to the merchant website and strengthen the link with this virtual environment. Based on this observation, it is desirable to integrate both technologies into the virtual market environment. While this study identified only two virtual reality devices, other technologies, such as instant messaging and personalized hosting, have not been mentioned and it would be interest-ing to investigate them in future studies. Indeed, the variety of these technologies offers designers of commercial websites a good leeway adapted to their budget constraints. Moreover, the effectiveness of virtual reality devices can vary from one context to another and depend on the category of products. Therefore, it would be relevant to study the condi-tions in which these technologies may be relevant. The research that could be suggested, also, for this study is to incite business leaders oper-ating online to implement an open innovation strategy. In fact, open innovation is a state of mind that is based on the sharing of expertise and that can be qualified as an accelerator of innovation within companies and businesses. Consequently, the open innovation strategy embodies the most revolutionary strategy whose objective is to adapt quickly to changes in the digital environment. It can give companies the opportunity to form strategic partnerships with companies specialized in the design of virtual anthropomorphic agents and commercial discussion forums. The advantage of this partnership for Tunisian companies is the reduction of costs, the access to a new technology and the acquiring of new knowledge and skills. In addition, for designers of virtual agents and commercial discussion forums, the ultimate advantage will be to access to growing markets. Open innovation induces a profound cultural change in the organizations; which can only be effective once investments and managerial support are at the height. Changing mentalities is a difficult task, but necessary to accompany a change approach. Companies surveyed must invest in human capital, process and training. The aim of these actions is to build a culture that is appropriate to open innovation and absorb external skills. As a result, companies must resort to recruiting new profiles and set up specialized training. These practices should be common to spread the culture of open innovation in any company. Given the exploratory nature of this research, the achieved conclusions may have generalization limits. This, however, deserves greater investigation in future quantitative studies, which would validate the various hypotheses identified in this work.

Conclusion

The notion of being "socially present" has gained a particular attention from researchers since the advent of ICTs. To better transmit the information and transform a support that is not user-friendly, several companies resort to ICTs to improve consumer's relations with the virtual merchant environment. Particularly, showing that the presence of virtual agent's influences the behavior toward websites (Ben Saad & Choura, 2013, 2016) is not enough anymore, it is now necessary and interesting to investigate the virtual reality devices that may improve the online shopping experience and make it more humane. In this qualitative study, we were able to identify two original devices: the anthropomorphic characteristics of the virtual agent and the characteristics of the commercial discussion forums. These tools reassure the user and would respectively affect the state of flow, the telepresence experience, the phenomenon of electronic word of mouth and the behavioral approach toward commercial websites. These tools enable the humanization of the human–machine interface. Moreover, these tools bring utilitarian and instrumental benefits for the Internet user who can meet with other visitors of the website to exchange information and find solutions to his problems. Other hedonic benefits of online escape can be cited like being a member of a discussion forum. We believe that social benefits also lend themselves to the experimental context with the presence of virtual reality devices. The social benefits refer to the needs of a social link with the members of the forum. In fact, the user can integrate a virtual community to fulfill a need for sociability. The results showed that the integration of ICTs as communication tools enhances community feelings and social presence. This work brings both theoretical and managerial contributions. It seems that it can provide answers to a recent research field that aims to understand the reactions of Internet users and their behavior on commercial websites.

Appendix

A set of screenshots illustrating the key features of the experimental website and the anthropomorphic virtual agent

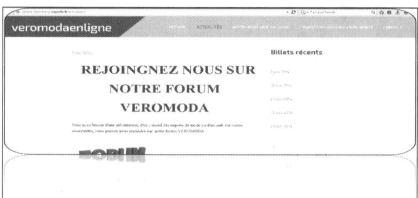

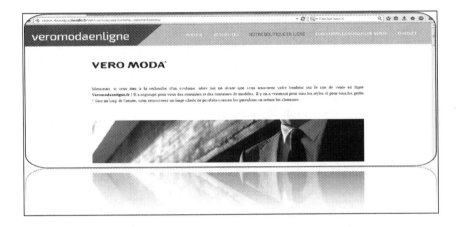

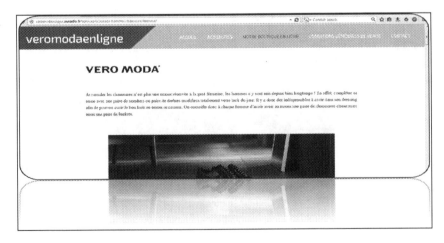

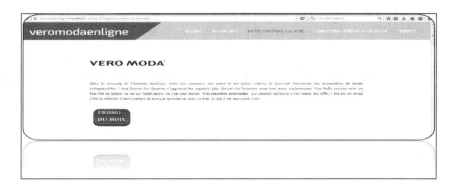

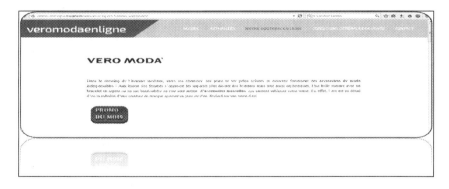

References

Allen, K., Racherla, P. & Buch, V. (2014). What we know and don't know about online word-of-mouth: A review and synthesis of the literature. *Journal of interactive Marketing*, 26(3), 167–183.

Almeida, S., Dholakia, U., Hermandez, J. & Mazzon, J. (2014). The mixed effects of participant diversity and expressive freedom in online peer-to-peer problem solving communities. *Journal of interactive Marketing*, 25 (3), 196–209.

Ardelet, C. & Brial, B. (2011). Influence of Internet users' recommendations: The role of social presence and expertise. *Research and Marketing Applications*, 3(1), 120–132.

Bush, V., King, R. & Racherla, P. (2014). What we know and don't know about electronic word-of-mouth: A systematic review and synthesis of the litera-ture. *Journal of Interactive Marketing*, 5(1), 133–147.

Baker, J. (1986). The role of environment in marketing services: The consumer perspective, in the services marketing challenge: integrated for competitive advantage. *American Marketing Association*, 21(5), 79–84.

Ben Saad, S. & Choura, F. (2013). The impact of social interactivity on the approach behavior of the Internet user: role of virtual agents. *International Conference Marketing Trends*, January 23–27, Paris.

Ben Saad, S. & Choura, F. (2016). Social interactivity and its impact on a user's approach behavior in commercial web sites: A study case of Virtual agent presence. *Journal of Marketing Management*, 2(4), 1–19.

Ben Saad, S. & Choura, F. (2017) Vers une meilleure compréhension de l'efficacité des dispositifs de réalité virtuelle sur les sites Web marchands: Etat des lieux et perspectives. *Revue française de marketing*, (article soumis).

Balbo, L., Jeannot, F. & Helme-Guison, A. (2013). Exploring the fit between jus-tification and social distance in consumers' responses to online-personalized recommendations. In: *32nd Advertising and Consumer Psychology Conference*, June 13–15, San Diego.

Bathelt, H. & Turi, P. (2011). Local, global and virtual buzz: The importance of face-to-face contact in economic interaction and possibilities to go beyond. *Journal of interactive Marketing*, 21(6), 520–529.

Blazevis, V., Wiertz, C., Cotte, J., Ruyter, K. & Isobel Keeling, D. (2014). GOSIP in cyberspace: Conceptualization and scale development for general online social interaction propensity. *Journal of Interactive Marketing*, 1(2), 87–100.

Bressoles, G. & Viot, C. (2014). The effects of a virtual agent on the personality and the quality of the site and the intentions of loyalty: Proposal of a concep-tual model. *8th International Congress Marketing Trends*, January 10–15, Venice.

Bressoles, G., Durrieu, F. & Senecal, S. (2014). A consumer typology-based on e-service quality and e-satisfaction. *International Journal of Retailing and Consumer Services*, 20(4), 889–896.

Charfi, A. (2012). The online experience immersion in virtual reality environments merchants, PhD Thesis, University of Paris-Dauphine, DRM-UMR CNRS 7088.

Charfi, A. & Volle, P. (2010). The immersive experience online: a new tool for commercial sites. French Marketing Journal, 234/235: 4–5 / 5.

Cook, W.A. (1994). Is it interactive media, or hyperactive media? *Journal of Advertising Research*, 2, 7–9.

Cyr, D., Hassanein, K., Head, M. & Ivaniv, A. (2007). The role of social presence in establishing loyalty in e-service environments. *Interacting with Computers*, 1, 43–56.

Csikszentmihalyi M. (1990). *Flow: The Psychology of Optimal Experience.* New York: Harper and Row.

Disbach, P.B., CHandon, J.L. & Galan, J.P. (2007). Effets de la présence et de la congruence d'un agent virtuel sur le pouvoir de rétention du site Internet. Actes du XXIIIème Congrès International de l'Association Française du Marketing, 11–16 Janvier, Aix-les-Bains.

Dolen, W., Dabholkar, P. & De Ruyter, J.C. (2007). *La satisfaction envers les discussions en ligne de clients: l'influence des attributes technologiques perçus, des caractéristiques du groupe de discussion et du style de communication du conseiller. Recherche et Applications en Marketing*, 1 (3), 83–112.

Evrard, Y., Pras, B. & Roux, E. (2009). Études *et recherches en marketing*, 4th edition. Paris: Dunod.

Garramone, H.A. & Anderson, L. (1986). The impacts of text-based cmc on online social presence. *Journal of Interactive Online Learning*, 21(1), 2–23.

Gensler, S., Volckner, Y.L. & Wiertz, C. (2013). Managing brands in the social media environment. *Journal of Interactive Marketing*, 20(4), 242–256.

Groth, M., Wu, Y., Nguyen, H. & Johnson, A. (2019). The moment of truth: A review, synthesis, and research agenda for the customer service experience. *Annual Review of Organizational Psychology and Organizational Behavior*, 6, 89–113.

Hoffman, D.L. & Novak, T.P. (2009). Flow online: lessons learned and future prospects. *Journal of Interactive Marketing*, 21(1), 23–34.

Huang S.-I. & Lin F.-R. (2007). The design and evaluation of an intelligent sales agent (ISA) for online persuasion and negotiation, *Electronic Commerce Research and Applications*, 6(1), 285–296.

Jamy, L. (2015). The benefit of being physically present: A survey of experimental works comparing co present robots, telepresent robots and virtual agents. *International Journal of Human–Computer Studies*, 23 (1), 23–37.

Jaureguiberry, F. & Proulx, S. (2017). *Usages et enjeux des technologies de communication*, Erès, Paris.

Labresque, L. (2014). Fostering consumer–brand relationships in social media environments: The role of parasocial interaction. *Journal of Interactive Marketing*, l2(1), 134–148.

Lemoine, J.-F. & Notebaert, J.F. (2011). Virtual agent and Internet users' confidence in a website. *Marketing Decisions*, 4, 47–53.

Lemoine, J.F. (2012). Looking for a better understanding of the behavior of Internet users. *Management and Future*, 58(1), 116–119.

Lemoine, J.F. & Cherif, E. (2015). Quel est le meilleur agent virtuel pour mon site? Une étude exploratoire des différentes caractéristiques anthropomorphiques, *XXXème Congrès International de l'Association Française du Marketing (AFM)*, 15 et 16 mai, Montpellier.

Lorna S., Maclaran P. & Brown S. (2019). An embodied approach to consumer experiences: the Hollister brandscape. *European Journal of Marketing*, 53(4), 806–828.

Mollen, A. & Wilson, H. (2010). Engagement, telepresence and interactivity in online consumer experience: reconciling scholastic and managerial perspectives. *Journal of Business Research*, 21(1), 919–25.

Nass, C., Lombard, M., Henriksen, L. and Steuer, J. (1995) Anthropocentrism and computers, *Behaviour and Information Technology*, 14(4), pp. 229–238.

Pelet, J.É., Ettis, S. & Cowart, K. (2014). Understanding optimal flow on time distortion in social media experience enhanced by telepresence. *19th AIM Symposium*, Aix-en-Provence, Provence: 19–21.

Sandelands, L.E. & Buckner, G.C. (1989). Aesthetic experience and the psychology of work feelings. *Research in Organizational Behavior*, 2(1), 105–131.

Steuer, J. (1992). Defining virtual reality: dimensions determining telepresence. *Journal of Communication*, 21(1), 73–93.

Steuer, J. & Nass, C.I. (1993) Voices, boxes and sources of messages computers and social actors, *Human Communication Research*, 19(4), 504–527.

Takahashi, T., Takeushi, Y. & Katagiri, Y. (2000). Change in human behaviours based on affiliation needs: toward the design of a social guide agent system. ATR Media Integration and Communications Research Laboratories, Working paper, Kyoto.

Thrau, T.H., Hofaker, C.F & Bloching, B. (2013). Marketing the pinball way: Understanding how social media change the generation of value for consumers and companies. *Journal of Interactive Marketing*, 4(1), 237–241.

Turkle, S. (1984) *The Second Self: Computers and the Human Spirit*. New York: Simon and Schuster.

Van Doorn, J., Mende, M., Noble, S.M., Hulland, J., Ostrom, A.L., Grewal, D. & Petersen, J.A. (2017). Domo arigato Mr. Roboto: Emergence of automated social presence in organizational frontlines and customers' service experiences. *Journal of Service Research*, 20(1), 43–58.

Voorveld *et al.* (2011). The relation between actual and perceived interactivity. *Journal of Advertising*, 40(2), 77–92.

Wang, L.C., Baker, J., Wagner, J.A. & Wakefield, K. (2007) Can a retail web site be social?, *Journal of Marketing*, 71(2), 143–157.

White, T., Novak, T.P. & Hoffman, D.L. (2014). No strings attached: When giving it away versus making them pay leads to negative net benefit perceptions in online exchanges. *Journal of Interactive Marketing*, 9(1), 96–121.

Zahao, Z., Salesse, R., Guergnon, M., Schmidt, R., Marin, L. & Bardy, B. (2015). Moving attractive virtual agent improves interpersonal coordination stability. *Human Movement Science*, 21(1), 240–254.

Chapter 10

Conclusion

Satyendra Singh[*,‡] and Luis Camacho[†,§]

University of Winnipeg, Winnipeg, MB R3B 2E9, Canada

†*SUNY Empire State College, Staten Island, NY 10305, USA*

‡*s.singh@uwinnipeg.ca*

§*luis.camacho@esc.edu*

This chapter concludes the book by summarizing all the chapters. In the lead chapter, findings of Hewett, Krasnikov and Hepworth support the notion that less developed institutional environments in emerging markets can negatively impact the overall intensity of international expansion by firms in those markets. In particular, high levels of corruption and less developed legal and judicial systems can reduce firms' abilities and/or willingness to embark on an intensive strategy for global expansion. However, their findings demonstrate mixed results in terms of how less developed institutional environments impact emerging markets firms' scope of expansion. The authors find that firms from more corrupt home markets submit applications to register their trademarks in fewer countries than firms from less corrupt home markets. However, stronger and more impartial legal systems also appear to impede the overall scope of firms' geographic expansion. The authors also find that when markets are high in corruption and the strength and impartiality of the legal systems are low, the overall level of trademark applications from those countries is lower.

In Japan, Chapter 3, Imagawa and Nakagawa present the theoretical implications of their research that fill the institutional voids in literature. Yakult's case suggests that if a company wants to be successful in an emerging market, it should prepare a similar business model that is effective and efficient. In the case of Yakult, their expatriate managers are educated in Japan regarding the operations of the Yakult Lady method for at least a few years before sending them to an emerging market to conduct business and learn about the local situation for more than 3 years. Afterward, the managers adjust the Yakult Lady method to be in line with the local situation. Using this active refinement approach to the Yakult Lady method, Yakult has been able to fully adapt to each emerging market's needs. Indeed, veteran expatriate managers who understand the company's way of doing business and the local market play a key role in business success in emerging markets.

In Chapter 4, Sarma, Matheus and Senaratne discuss the influence and recent developments of AI and cyber security in emerging economies and build a framework of key elements of AI and cyber security that would positively influence the knowledge economy of emerging markets, leading to improved outputs as well as increased income and consumption. For future research, they intend to explore the uncertainty surrounding the future shaping of AI tools and techniques, in particular intelligent agents and disruptive technology that combine other disciplines. The policy implications for developing economies are multi-fold; for example, the rise of legal issues around AI and cyber security, ideological and ethical concerns, public perception, impact on workforce and economic issues. These policy gaps require attention and solutions that take into consideration the rapidly evolving landscape of AI and cyber security.

In Croatia in Chapter 5, Čižmešija and Škrinjarić show that monthly CS data on variables relating to financial situation of consumers could be used to model and forecast yearly data on the poverty rates. The authors use the MIDAS regression analysis and suggest the following recommendations for policymakers. First, in order to reduce the poverty within a country, a monitoring system that can quantify and accurately forecast the important variables needs to be constructed. However, the timing of such activities needs to be in accordance with the needs and limitations of the policymakers and managers involved in the process. The authors focus on the methodological aspect of obtaining the results quickly compared to the usual approaches of annual surveys and indices construction which provide data with lags. Further, using the data is cheaper than obtaining data from specialized institutions as the data used in this study were freely available, which is another advantage of using MIDAS regression.

In the context of China, in Chapter 6, Yang, Zhou, Chen and Carney conclude that innovation inputs (actors) tend to affect incremental innovation more than radical innovation in China. This raises the question of what motivates these actors to pursue incremental innovation within the Chinese institutional ecosystem. The significant negative impact of FDI on innovation capacity further suggests that increasing FDI alone does not improve the innovation capacity of a region. Policymakers should consider developing infrastructure to enable Chinese firms and institutions to reap the benefits of positive technology spillovers from foreign companies, as simply attracting FDI alone does not lead to those benefits. As a result, the government needs to devise proper policies to create an ecosystem to effectively utilize FDI for the purposes of regional innovation capacity development.

In Latin American countries of Peru, Chile and Argentina, Beamond, Farndale and Hartel in Chapter 7 infer that talent management strategies of multinational enterprises (MNEs) with operations in emerging economies may need to adapt to complex local factors that influence the motivation, satisfaction and loyalty of local talent. According to the authors, there is, however, a concurrent need to adopt corporate headquarters' strategies across all organizational levels through a process of translation, responding to both globalization and localization needs simultaneously. MNEs with operations in emerging markets economies need to work on strategies that cover local talent skills shortages, retention strategies and stiff competition for valuable talent.

In Chapter 8, Robles and Klarner conclude that a business incubator (BI) may impact the development of management control systems (MCSs) in start-ups mainly in two ways. First, it may push the start-ups toward a non-traditional conceptualization of MCSs beyond organizational borders, focusing specifically on stakeholders such as freelancers and clients. Second, BIs may train a start-up on how to create credibility toward external investors. A BI can thus increase the awareness and initiative of entrepreneurs to implement stronger MCSs before applying to venture capital (VC). The authors further suggest that incubation processes do not intentionally make it their goal to create strong MCSs in start-ups. But by consciously choosing to train entrepreneurs in the design of MCSs and by highlighting MCSs' benefits, BIs may increase the survival rates of the incubated start-ups and VC may become more accessible for them.

In the final chapter, Saad and Choura suggest that information and communication technologies are important to improve consumer's relations with the virtual merchant environment. In this context, the authors identify two factors: the anthropomorphic characteristics of the virtual agent and the characteristics of the commercial discussion forums. The authors conclude that social benefits — the need of a social link with the members of the forum — lend themselves to the experimental context with the presence of virtual reality devices and that integration of ICTs as communication tools enhances community feelings and social presence.

Index

Printed in the United States
By Bookmasters